Democracy and the Ethical Life

Democracy and the Ethical Life

A Philosophy of Politics and Community

Second Edition, Expanded

Claes G. Ryn

The Catholic University of America Press
Washington, D.C.

Copyright © 1990 Claes G. Ryn
All rights reserved
Printed in the United States of America

First published by Louisiana State University Press

Library of Congress Cataloging-in-Publication Data
Ryn, Claes G., 1943–
    Democracy and the ethical life : a philosophy of politics and
community / by Claes G. Ryn.—2nd ed., expanded.
        p.   cm.
    1. Political ethics.   2. Democracy.   3. Representative govern-
ment and representation.   I. Title.
JA79.B93   1990
321.8—dc20   89-27784
ISBN 0-8132-0711-8

Contents

Prefatory Note for the 1990 Edition   vii

Acknowledgments   ix

PART ONE: Democracy as an Ethico-Philosophical Problem

I   Democracy and Man's Moral Predicament   3
    Democracy as a Way of Life   16
    Morality and Self-Interest   20

II   Human Experience and the "Scientific Method"   27
    Self-Awareness   36
    The Human Frame of Reference   42

PART TWO: The Ethical Life

III   The Duality of Human Nature   52
    The Logic of Participation   60
    The Higher and the Lower Self   62
    Ethical Conscience as Censure and Purpose   69
    The Paradox of Moral Freedom   73
    Morality as Happiness   75

IV   The Ethics of Community   81
    The Ethical Life and Tradition   87

PART THREE: Rousseau's General Will: Moral Fact or Utopian Fiction?

V   The Political Moralism of Rousseau   92
    Rousseau the Man and the Thinker   97

VI   The Rebirth of Nature   102
     Equality or Slavery   *108*
     Social Freedom   *111*

VII The General Will   117
     The General Will and Representation   *120*
     The Rejection of Constitutionalism   *127*
     The Spontaneity of the Moral Will   *131*
     The Unity of the State   *138*
     Nationalism and Military Virtue   *141*

VIII Utopian Dreams and Harsh Realities   146

     PART FOUR: The Ethics of Constitutional
     Democracy

IX   Constitutionalism and Popular Sovereignty   154
     The American Constitution   *154*
     The Idea of Popular Sovereignty   *160*

X   The Spirit of Constitutionalism   166

XI   Constitutionalism versus Plebiscitarianism   182
     Decentralization   *194*
     "Democratization"   *196*

XII Democracy, Leadership, and Culture   199

     PART FIVE: A Postscript

XIII The Common Good and History   206
     The Particularity of Ethical Good   *210*
     The Ethics of Freedom and Diversity   *218*
     The Good as Historically Evolving   *223*
     Ethical Realism   *229*

XIV The State of Democracy   232

     Index   241

Prefatory Note for the 1990 Edition

This edition of *Democracy and the Ethical Life* retains the text of the original edition published by Louisiana State University Press. Except for correcting some printing and editing errors, I have resisted the temptation to revise the old chapters. A new section, "Part Five: A Postscript," has been added to this edition, and there are related changes in the index and table of contents.

Claes G. Ryn

Washington, D.C.
November, 1989

Acknowledgments

In writing this book I have benefited from contacts with many individuals. I owe a large debt of gratitude to René de Visme Williamson. He has given very generously of his learning, wisdom, and personal warmth. In a sense of the word *representative* that he would recognize, he is truly a representative Christian scholar. To my friend Folke Leander, a penetrating and creative philosopher and also a great teacher, go my deep-felt thanks for having contributed more than I can say to the solution of philosophical problems that are at the core of this book. I am indebted in numerous ways to Russell Kirk. His books have profoundly influenced my outlook ever since I made them extra-curricular reading as a young student at the University of Uppsala in Sweden. Several years later it was becoming clear that my rejection of positivism and moral relativism, which have a monopoly in Swedish academic circles, would seriously impair, not to say preclude, a career of scholarship in my own country. With his usual kindness Kirk then offered some invaluable advice about coming to the United States. For this I am most genuinely thankful. It brought me into contact with René de Visme Williamson and led to the continuation of my academic work in a very hospitable country with room for more than one school of thought. Many others have my gratitude for ideas, advice, and support.

Although I have drawn heavily on many thinkers past and present, their ideas have been absorbed here into an argument of my own. Needless to say, I alone must bear the blame for the possible shortcomings of the synthesis presented in this book.

Claes G. Ryn

Washington, D.C.
July, 1977

PART ONE

Democracy as an Ethico-Philosophical Problem

Democracy and Man's Moral Predicament

1

The prevalent tendency among modern political theorists is
to define democracy without reference to a transcendent
ethical standard. Democracy is usually treated as a kind of
procedural form, neutral in regard to the substance of the
popular will. It is viewed as a "method" for making public decisions, a *modus procedendi* in Joseph Schumpeter's phrase. [1]
This form of government, it is argued, does not imply a presumption in favor of any particular set of values beyond that
which is necessarily embodied in the rules and rights which
constitute democracy. In fact, democracy is sometimes regarded as the form of government which recognizes the im-
possibility of demonstrating the inherent superiority of one
scale of values over another. This view has been succinctly
stated by Hans Kelsen: "He who holds that absolute truth and
absolute values are beyond human understanding is forced to
look upon a rival alien opinion as possible at the very least.

1 For some variations on this general theme, see Joseph Schumpeter,
Capitalism, Socialism and Democracy (New York: Harper and Row, 1950);
Henry B. Mayo, *An Introduction to Democratic Theory* (New York: Oxford Uni-
versity Press, 1960); E. F. M. Durbin, *The Politics of Democratic Socialism*
(London: Routledge & Kegan Paul, 1940); David Easton, *The Political System*
(New York: Alfred A. Knopf, 1971); David Truman, *The Governmental Process*
(New York: Alfred A. Knopf, 1971); Robert Dahl, *A Preface to Democratic
Theory* (Chicago: University of Chicago Press, 1956); Anthony Downs, *An
Economic Interpretation of Democracy* (New York: Harper & Bros., 1957).

Relativism is therefore the Philosophy (Weltanschauung) which the democratic conception presupposes." [2] Without passing moral judgment on anyone, except possibly the antidemocratic, democracy provides the framework for the peaceful settlement of disputes.

This type of reasoning about democracy bears a certain resemblance and appears intimately related to the view of political theory which Arnold Brecht calls "scientific value relativism." [3] According to that doctrine, which incorporates the attempted dichotomy between "facts" and "values," scientific work is ethically neutral. While it is recognized by those who adopt this view that devotion to science and its methods involves some sort of moral commitment, they deny that science as such has any ultimate moral purpose. It is a way of proceeding, a method of inquiry which may serve men with very different values. Political theory proper does not attempt to establish the moral superiority of one scale of values over another, for all scientific claims have to be intelligible to the community of scholars, and we do not have access to an objective, communicable order of values. All we have access to by scientific means, as defined by Brecht, are the subjective preferences of individuals.

The similarities between the doctrine of scientific value relativism and much modern democratic theory are thus apparent. Both attempt to separate method from ultimate end. That is not to say that the analogy between the dominant view of democracy and the mentioned conception of science is

2 Hans Kelsen, *Allgemeine Staatslehre* (Berlin: Springer, 1925), 370. Quoted and translated in René de Visme Williamson, "The Challenge of Political Relativism," *Journal of Politics*, IX (May, 1947), 150.
3 The term "scientific value relativism" is used by Arnold Brecht in *Political Theory: The Foundation of Twentieth Century Political Thought* (Princeton: Princeton University Press, 1959). The book contains an extensive explication of the doctrine.

complete—it is not—only that there appears to be considerable cross-fertilization. It can be said about both that they exhibit a fundamental ambiguity, growing out of a failure to come to grips with basic problems of ethics and logic. Although most academic defenders of the "procedural" view of democracy and scientific value relativism admit that they must ultimately justify their preference for democracy and science by falling back on a value judgment, they claim to ascribe to their systems no overriding purpose or predetermined goal. Among the theorists of democracy, this point is emphatically made by Henry B. Mayo:

Democracy sets up no scientifically ascertained "end" for man, has no all-consuming purpose, no Form of the Good, no final ultimate to serve. It has its operating principles and their values; it has the values inherent in the system; and it has a typical character which it both presupposes and promotes. Within these limits a democracy may be used to pursue aims which change from time to time. . . . The realm of political and social purposes in a democracy is open and indeterminate.[4]

The difficulty with this statement, and any analogous statement about science, is that we are asked to picture the good democrat as one who places a high value on certain procedural rules which together are supposed to form a democracy, but who does so with no ulterior motive in mind. It is not easy to grasp what meaning there would be in a value judgment which expresses a liking for democratic procedures but does not also imply an endorsement of some ultimate goal, such as the achievement of civilization or happiness. The postulation of the existence of this type of value judgment would seem to involve a distinction between ends and means of very doubtful validity. As is persuasively argued by John Dewey, ends have to be viewed as constituted by the means

4 Mayo, *Democratic Theory*, 277.

chosen for their attainment. Conversely, means are a partial fulfillment of ends. "Ends" and "means," in other words, are only two ways of looking at the same process of continuous purposive activity. In Dewey's formulation: "'End' is a name for a series of acts taken collectively . . . 'Means' is a name for the same series taken distributively."[5] The methods of democracy, thus, cannot be distinguished from the consequences, whether immediate and expected or distant and unforeseen, which are implied in and promoted by those methods. Mayo is not completely oblivious to this idea, but he fails to see that it calls into question his whole approach to democracy.

How else could democratic rules acquire value for a person than by contributing to what he understands, with or without justification, to be the final value of life? It is of course possible to endorse a certain set of means with only an incomplete or mistaken view of its effects, but to the extent that our choice is not completely irrational, that set of means must be assumed by us to be conducive to the goal which in the end makes life worth living. Mayo admits that democratic procedures promote certain values. By that token, we might add, they also counteract the realization of other values, notably many of those advocated by Communists or Nazis. Can it be argued at the same time that democracy leaves the final goal of life open? Conversely, if it is true that as good democrats we must view the end of life as completely undetermined, by what logic are we favoring certain political arrangements over others?

To argue in response, for instance, that democratic procedures require or imply no ultimate end, but receive the only justification needed from the fact that they give the individ-

5 John Dewey, *Human Nature and Conduct* (New York: Modern Library, 1957), 35.

ual a measure of freedom to pursue his own goals, partly by giving him some control over public policy, is to have missed the point of this argument, which is that *freedom, goal, control*, etc., if they are not to be empty slogans, have to be defined with reference to a value conceived as ultimate. Insofar as the procedural means of democracy are intelligently chosen, that end is implied in, indeed, partially fulfilled by them. Mayo and other theorists with a similar view of democracy are assuming considerably more about the proper goal for man than they are clearly aware of.

Only if we have some idea, however vague or confused, of the intrinsic worth of things, can we maintain the sense of direction and proportion without which existence would become meaningless, all science pointless. Science presupposes not only order in the universe but the value of discovering that order. Instead of facing squarely the possibility that men's ethical concerns, as reflected for instance in an affirmation of democratic rights and the pursuit of truth, have a common focus and that there is an awareness of the good for man which transcends the subjective biases of individuals and groups and which can be examined scientifically, the scholar who accepts scientific value relativism establishes residence in a philosophical halfway house. There he can entertain a certain scale of values, and thus give some meaning and coherence to life, without ever having to examine its final tenability, without in a sense ever having to accept responsibility for it. By labeling all statements of "ultimate values" subjective, he ends inquiry into their validity before it has had a chance to begin. And he does not manage to keep science ethically neutral in return, but only makes it easier to introduce value preferences in an uncritical manner.

The word *democracy* is both one of the most used and one of the most abused terms in modern Western political dis-

course. It may be argued that the corresponding theoretical
confusion is partly the result of the vast influence of some
kind of ethical relativism or nihilism. Having rejected the belief in a definite, enduring purpose for human life, democratic theorists have a difficult time establishing a common
point of reference. The doors are open for a raid on the democratic vocabulary. The aim of this study is to contribute to a
restoration of theoretical and terminological clarity about
democracy by relating it to man's quest for the moral life. In
choosing that approach I join the philosophical tradition
founded in the West by Plato and Aristotle. An attempt will
be made to develop an ethical interpretation of democracy,
that is, one which takes its sense of direction and proportion
from an ethico-philosophical understanding of man's nature
and destiny, and states the implications of that understanding for popular government. Rather than start with a ready-
made definition of democracy and then look for its moral
prerequisites, I shall try to decide how popular self-rule
needs to be designed in order to support the ethical life. If the
demands of ethics are to be taken seriously, this would seem
to be putting the horse before the cart.

Ethics will not be regarded as confined to the study of inherently subjective claims about the end of human life. It
will be assumed that man is able to go beyond the relative and
subjective in morals, and that philosophy can give an account
of this process. By ethical conscience will be understood, not
some arbitrary, merely private or conventional principle of
conduct, but the awareness, stronger in some people than in
others, that there is a sacred purpose to human life which
transcends the transitory biases of individuals and peoples,
and which can be violated only at the price of a loss of meaning and worth. Ethical conscience is that in man which wills,
not the private advantage of individuals or groups as an end in

itself, but the realization of the universal good for man. Ethical philosophy seeks to describe the nature of this ordering principle. To avoid misunderstanding, it should be said that ethical philosophy is trying to give ever clearer intellectual expression to a sense of spiritual direction which in the end defies all specific formulations. By ethical conscience I mean a special grasp of reality, dynamically related to, but transcendent of, rationality. What is absolute in man's ethical life, therefore, is not this or that standard of conduct which he formulates in response to the ethical demand on him, but the moral obligation itself, the imperative of always *looking* for the self-justifying solution in the particular situation. Some Christians would perhaps prefer to say that ethical conscience is the Holy Spirit revealing itself to man. To use that terminology would have the advantage of ruling out unfortunate references to the loose and slippery meaning of the word *conscience* in common parlance. It would also make the intended association with divine purpose clearer. On the other hand, it would probably unnecessarily complicate acceptance of my analysis by those who are unable to accept the specifically Christian notion of God.

To state adequately the reasons for rejecting ethical relativism and nihilism and siding with the classical tradition in ethics started by Plato and Aristotle and the closely related Judaeo-Christian tradition would be ample material for a separate work. It is necessary here to refer to other scholars who continue those traditions. Although this older frame of reference collides at important points with some widely held modern beliefs, the writer who regards it as valid in central respects cannot always begin from the ground, so to speak, by defending its basic assumptions against the most recent attacks. To be able to make his own contribution to these old traditions by suggesting clarifications, revisions, developments, or new applications of their ideas, he must be allowed to build on the base which has been laid by others. At the same time, the value of scholarly exchange makes it desirable that arguments be presented in such a way as to be meaningful and plausible also to those with a different frame of reference. I hope that in the course of the proposed inquiry into the relationship of ethical conscience to popular self-rule a persuasive case for the implied view of ethics will also be developed.

The introduction of an ethical perspective on popular government will force the rethinking of democratic principles as widely understood by political scientists today. An ethical theory of democracy will not be satisfied with stating, for instance, that democracy is a form of government in which public policy rests on the will of the great mass of the people as opposed to some privileged elite. While this principle has something to contribute to a theory of popular rule, it evades the question whether democracy has to foster a certain quality of popular will. An ethical theory of democracy looks for more in the celebrated principle of majority rule than the idea that a numerically superior portion of a people is entitled to greater influence over public decisions than a numerically inferior one. As stated, the principle leaves the demands of ethics aside. The same type of deficiency marks most influential modern theories of democracy. In search of the "basic feature" of this form of government, Henry Mayo decides upon the following criterion: "A political system is democratic to the extent that the decision-makers are under effective popular control." [6] There is of course more to Mayo's definition of democracy, but the fact that he regards this as the "basic feature" is a good illustration of the tendency in mod-

6 Mayo, *Democratic Theory*, 60.

ern democratic theory to view this type of government as a mere form in which may be put almost any substance. There is contained in this allegedly fundamental criterion no reference to the quality of will which democracy is supposed to articulate, but only this formula: the more popular control, the more democracy. Once again we are left with a definition that does little more than place democracy on a quantitative scale.

Of course, Henry B. Mayo is only one of the large number of contemporary theorists who have taken on the difficult task of defining democracy. One would have to simplify a great deal even to regard him as representative of the vast majority who deny the possibility of adjusting the definition to an ascertainable universal standard of good. There are as many theories of popular rule as there are theorists. One hesitates to place in any one category authors as diverse as, for instance, Robert Dahl, Anthony Downs, Alf Ross, Giovanni Sartori, Thomas Landon Thorson, and Herbert Tingsten. It is not necessary for our purposes to deal specifically with their ideas, valuable though many of them are in understanding democracy. What stands out about them in our present perspective is a fundamental weakness, the failure to relate popular government to man's transcendent moral destiny. Because of this flaw, these theorists, although quite different in other respects, tend to gravitate in the direction of some form of proceduralism. In that limited sense, we may perhaps be allowed to view Mayo as a roughly representative figure.

Although considerable sophistication sometimes goes into the procedural type of definition, the fundamental question is left unanswered. What is the ultimate justification for the procedures that are endorsed? However skillful in some ways, defenses of constitutionalism in this vein fall short of show-

ing that this form of government does not just serve some
mysteriously derived "preference," but is a moral necessity
growing out of the very nature of man.

It should be mentioned that some of the contemporary
theorists leaning in the direction of a procedural definition
are at least partially aware of the difficulties with the
means-end distinction. Thorson, for instance, sounds much
like John Dewey when he writes: "Any careful examination
of ethics will surely show that there is no clear-cut distinction between means and ends, between what is done and how
it is done—that is, between method and substance."[7] This
insight is potentially no mean improvement on Mayo's reasoning, but it does not appear to lead beyond Dewey or even to
the limits of Dewey's philosophy. In fact, despite the latter's
stated denials of a transcendent standard of good, one may
well ask if there is not in his philosophy an implicit appreciation of such a standard which is stronger than in most contemporary social scientists who have been influenced by his
ideas. Important parts of Dewey's thought actually seem to
invite revision with reference to an ethical philosophy similar
to my own. It can be meaningful indeed to view democracy as
a set of procedures. But not only is it then necessary to recognize that those procedures are but one way of looking at a
concrete substance, as Dewey would point out; that substance is also a partial realization or violation of a transcendent moral standard.

Modern democratic theory also has its rebels. Among those
who have made notable contributions to the reconstruction of
this field of inquiry in the light of ethics are John Hallowell,
Walter Lippmann, John Courtney Murray, Reinhold Niebuhr, and René de Visme Williamson, to mention only a few

7 Thomas Landon Thorson, *The Logic of Democracy* (New York: Holt, Rinehart
and Winston, 1962), 149.

distinguished Americans who have dealt specifically with the problems of popular rule. It will not be necessary here to evaluate their writings in detail, but I should indicate my sympathy with their effort to deal with democracy as it relates to the possibility of reconciling politics with man's higher destiny.

As soon as the demands of the ethical life are recognized, it becomes necessary to find out how government could be made to respect those demands. How can moral values be promoted and maintained by a form of government based on popular consent? Jean-Jacques Rousseau, who is widely regarded as one of the fathers of modern democracy, finds the answer in his concept of the general will. The latter is by definition always moral, and it is the only legitimate expression of the people's will. To make government moral it is necessary to create the circumstances under which the general will can assert itself. It is important to note that Rousseau regards the general will as incompatible with constitutional restraints on the people. He does so because he associates morality with uninhibited spontaneity. The cause of the good society is not threatened by man's first impulse, which is always good, but by the artificial motives with which historical society has imprisoned and perverted his natural, original goodness. Constitutional checks on the will of the people are examples of such vitiating influences. In order for man's spontaneous sense of right to break forth, they have to be removed, together with all other artificial restraints which bind his natural goodness. This, in brief, is the ethical philosophy behind Rousseau's notion of plebiscitary democracy.

Rousseau's view of how morality is to be served in politics differs fundamentally from the thesis that will be advanced in this study. It will be contended here that the idea of democracy, viewed as a realistic statement of human potentiality, is at the same time the idea of constitutional democracy, that is, of popular rule under legal restraints not easily changed. This is so because of the nature of man's moral predicament. The argument will be developed partly through an analysis of Rousseau's concept of the general will. His thought deserves careful examination, for not only has it had an enormous influence, directly and indirectly, on democratic theory and political thought generally in the West; it also takes one to the root of problems which have to be faced and solved before the present confusion in democratic theory can be overcome. While Rousseau deserves credit for raising the moral question of popular rule, it may be shown that on the whole his influence has been detrimental. He is the great pioneer in the West for the type of ethics which identifies the principle of moral good with positive human feelings, a morality of the "heart" from which the West has yet to recover. It is this understanding of ethics which lies at the bottom of his impatience with inner or outer restraints on man. I shall try to show that the general will, for which Rousseau claims total power and freedom, is not what it is purported to be, a principle of right above subjective and particular wills.

It will be argued here that man's ethical conscience is not adequately defined as a positive force inside our impulsive life. It is better described as a principle of self-examination or censure set apart from particular human feelings and actions. Except in a special sense, it does not order this or that specific line of conduct. It alters the *motive* with which action is contemplated. Human impulse is never itself the standard of morality. It may be said to partake of that standard to the extent that it advances the transcendent purpose known in ethical conscience.

This moral principle of self-examination can be shown to be closely related to the idea of constitutionalism. A constitution and other laws is a check on human will. In a democracy where constitutional provisions, whether written or unwritten, regulate popular voting, representation, terms of office, divisions of power, legislative procedure, etc., and these rules can be changed only with sustained effort, arbitrariness and whim in the people at large and in their representatives are restrained. Such a government does not give free rein to the people's impulse of the moment, but requires of public decisions that they be reached in a certain deliberate way.

In a democracy, constitutional checks may be viewed as inhibitions imposed by a people and its representatives on themselves. But why would a people restrict its own freedom of action? Rousseau completely rejects this idea of government. Constitutionalism involves a distrust of unhampered action and spontaneous decision. These are regarded as containing an element of arbitrariness destructive of the spirit of the civilized political order. One purpose of constitutional law, and lesser laws, is to purge government as far as possible of this element and to create the conditions for reasoned, well-considered public decisions. The attempt to make room for critical detachment in the formulation of policy may have an ethical aspect. Where there is room for deliberation, there is room for the application of a moral perspective. It is my thesis that in one of its aspects constitutionalism is the political dimension of ethical self-restraint and hence the necessary political condition for the furtherance of the ethical life. The idea of constitutional democracy, as opposed to the Rousseauistic notion of plebiscitary democracy, can be viewed as implying a recognition on the part of the people that there is a need to protect ourselves from our own spontaneity in politics. We need to be on our guard against premature, unthinking inclinations and the selfish arbitrariness which usually lurks behind them. Just as an individual may resolve on the basis of experience of his own moral weakness not to give free rein to his impulses in the future, but to make room for moral scrutiny of his motives before acting, so a people may recognize the need for putting brakes on its own momentary will in the interest of the common good.

Nothing in formal logic as taught today stops a thinker from advancing a theory of democracy in which the need for constitutional checks is denied or discounted. The question, however, is if it must not then be regarded as belonging to the realm of futile and potentially dangerous dreams. One may argue that such a theory becomes palatable only when certain traits of human nature are assumed to be not really a part of man's being. Specifically, such a theory makes light of man's moral predicament, which may be described as the permanent inner tension between ethical conscience and contrary inclinations.

Democracy as a Way of Life

In the following attempt to give an ethical interpretation of democracy it will not be taken for granted that democracy is inherently superior to all other forms of government, as is often done by modern Westerners. It is well to remember Aristotle's observation that no one type of government is suited to all circumstances. It is pointless to argue in the abstract that only democratic governments are legitimate. As John Stuart Mill points out, "A people may be unwilling or unable to fulfill the duties which a particular form of government requires of them." [8] The question of the legitimacy of different types of rule should not be discussed in isolation from the cultural context to which they belong. Democracy may be a realistic proposition in Europe or North America, but on the African continent most peoples still seem to lack the special type of political maturity which is needed to sus-

8 John Stuart Mill, *Utilitarianism, Liberty and Representative Government* (London: J. M. Dent & Sons, 1929), 178.

tain it. In the West of today, where democracy has come to be viewed as the normal form of government, it should be remembered that historically and internationally democracy, in a meaningful sense of that word, is not the rule but the exception. We should be on our guard lest we adopt a provincial or superficial attitude in regard to the means whereby a society may provide for its political needs.

At the same time, there are strong reasons why the idea of democracy must be regarded as a very noble one. A good case can be made that in a certain sense it represents the apex of associated human life. This argument relates democracy to the moral end of man, introducing the image of popular self-government in the cause of community. Without assenting to his entire political philosophy, we may quote these pregnant lines by John Dewey: "Regarded as an idea, democracy is not an alternative to other principles of associated life. It is the idea of community life itself. It is an ideal in the only intelligible sense of an ideal: namely, the tendency and movement of some thing which exists carried to its final limit, viewed as completed, perfected." Clearly, the word democracy is used by Dewey in a much broader sense than a set of political institutions and rules. It refers to the sum of conditions which prevail in a society where community has been realized. Certain political arrangements form only a part of a more comprehensive design. The word *democracy* implies that the active involvement of the whole people is necessary for the achievement of the goal of community. It should be added without delay that according to Dewey "democracy in this sense is not a fact and never will be." [9] We may understand him to be using the term in an Aristotelian fashion: something is what it is potentially.

Dewey's broadening of the democratic concept to denote a

9 John Dewey, *The Public and Its Problems* (Chicago: Swallow Press, 1954), 148.

whole way of life with a definite end puts him at loggerheads with theorists who regard democracy as a mere political form without any overriding purpose. He would seem to be more sensitive than they are to the fact that government derives its shape, strength, and direction from the aspirations of the people it serves. It will reflect and promote the ultimate goals for life that are held by that people and its leaders. Except in a loose empirical way, one cannot really define a form of government by abstract principles, such as universal suffrage, popular control of government officials, and majority rule, for these take on different meanings depending on the social ethos that pervades them. A political institution is not some kind of distinct phenomenon, but is constituted by the quality of the acts of those who administer it and of those who respect its authority. These acts are a manifestation of a certain cultural atmosphere, of the "regime," to speak with Aristotle. By defining democracy in terms of community, Dewey ascribes to popular rule a definite goal with reference to which its various procedural rules must be understood.

Dewey's broad definition of democracy brings up the artificiality of all attempted sharp distinctions between public and private life. The political scientist needs to make distinctions along that line, for they are useful to him in organizing his thought and in communicating his ideas to others. But while it may be *practical* for some purposes to define the casting of a vote by a legislator as a public act and the disciplining of a child by a parent as a private act, it should not be forgotten that this distinction is, in the final analysis, arbitrary. The label "public" is tacked on to the first, not because it is somehow *sui generis*, but because it pertains to "government" as conventionally understood and because it has a direct and powerful effect on the lives of many other people. One need only change the example of the "private" act to one in which the effect on others is both direct and powerful to find it even more difficult to draw the line. It may perhaps be said that an act is public as opposed to private to the extent that it affects the lives of other people, but that formula involves no sharp distinction, only a diffuse sliding scale.[10]

It is thus in a sense unreal to think of "government" as something distinct from a surrounding "society." It is, or becomes, what the total number of "private" and "public" acts make it. It is impossible to determine with any finality where the "rules" and "institutions" of democracy end and the cultural "environment" begins. They are dynamically related. They are parts of one and the same process of purposeful human action.

Dewey's idea of community suffers from certain philosophical difficulties which make it impossible to adopt many of the specifics of his view of popular rule. Still, his notion that democracy carries within it the idea of community is a valuable one. It suggests that popular self-government has a built-in moral requirement and logical end which cannot be ignored if this form of rule is to continue in existence. Although it is not my purpose to prove that democracy is "the idea of community life itself," the analysis will point in that direction. I shall be trying to show that the ethical quest to which democracy owes allegiance is the quest for community, to borrow Robert Nisbet's phrase.[11] Needless to say, the idea of community as the goal to which politics should be directed is central to the classical and Judaeo-Christian tradition.

10 To avoid misunderstanding it should perhaps be said that in introducing the notion that democracy implies a whole way of life I am not also moving in the direction of the idea that all decisions which have "public" ramifications should be made according to majority rule or some other principle of "participatory" democracy.

11 See Robert Nisbet, *Community and Power* (New York: Oxford University Press, 1962).

How this idea is to be understood and related to the concept of popular government will have to be discussed in some detail. Ethical conscience, I argue, pulls man in the opposite direction from the centrifugal forces of subjective bias, arbitrariness, and egotism. It may be described as a sense of belonging, as participation in a harmonizing, supraindividual purpose. Given man's contrary proclivities, the only type of popular self-rule which can serve that goal in the political realm is a constitutional one.

Morality and Self-Interest

The emphasis in this study will be on the ethical aspect of the problem of democracy. It would not be surprising if in the course of such an investigation the impression emerges that morality is *the* source of order in a democracy. To avoid creating that impression, some cautionary and sobering remarks should be made.

Human nature, as we know it so far in history and in ourselves, does not give any reasons for optimism about the triumph of ethical motives over selfish motives in human affairs. Respect for the ethical goal of life does not seem to be the rule of politics but the exception. Some political philosophers, Machiavelli and Hobbes prominent among them, have been so overwhelmed by the element of raw power in politics that they have been able to see almost nothing else. Hobbes is even led to the drastic step of redefining morals in terms of the urge for power. However great their exaggerations, these philosophers have driven home an important truth which must not be ignored by anyone who studies politics and particularly not by anyone who wants to do so in the light of ethics: politics is primarily an arena of conflict, of clashing individual wills and group interests. One may go a step further and say that life in general has an element of war, of which military conflicts and other forms of violence are only one type of manifestation. A basic role of government is to provide for the peaceful settlement of disputes. Laws, including constitutions, have the function of steering the perpetual war of all against all into forms which can make life tolerable. Of this function of government modern theorists of democracy are often quite aware. In the United States, the Madisonian tradition makes it difficult to forget that constitutions have as an important aim the checking and balancing of conflicting interests. The realism of Madison's insights are attested to by the success of the American constitutional experiment.

There is thus much to be learned from those who are sensitive to the clash of wills that forms a part of all political life. The trouble with that type of observation is that it often sees *nothing* in politics but the war of all against all. When government is conceived as based on nothing but a prudential, pragmatic effort to settle disputes peacefully, when the ethical perspective is pushed aside or dropped entirely, the result is a distortion of political reality. It is forgotten that while regulation of conflict may be the first and foremost task of government, citizens have an ethical conscience which demands more. Man's moral aspirations, too, are a part of political life. Although these may not often triumph over the demands of the power play, they are there to give a sense of higher direction to politics, to smooth the rough edges of the war of wills, at rare times even to raise government to a level of some moral dignity.

Man's ethical conscience is not *the* ordering principle of politics, not even in a democracy, but it does pull our will in the direction of worthier political goals, limiting to some degree their ingredient of mere selfishness. Insofar as it gains influence, we may say that the good society is being realized. In that society, which we can also call the civilized society, selfishness has not been uprooted. One might say that it has been tamed, bent to the purposes of the moral life. Where man's awareness of the ethical goal of life recedes, on the other hand, the ever-present power struggle will soon assume uglier forms, giving new support to a cynically Machiavellian view of politics.

An ethical theory of democracy, then, must not blind itself to the powerful and inescapable role of nonethical motives in politics. These forces must be taken into account by the realistic theorist as well as the prudent politician. If the politician is to be successful in attaining his goals, he must try to adjust to these forces, try to enlist them in his support. That is not to say that he has to be immoral and opportunistic, only that he must not be naïve about his working material. He may have a deeply moral view of his duty as a politician, but if he refuses to face up to the degree to which nonmoral motives are among the forces with which he has to contend, he will be reduced to a futile moralism which may even produce the opposite of the intended results. It is not moral, but merely foolish, to ignore the more unpleasant political drives. It can even be said that it is a moral duty for the politician to adjust his means to the circumstances, that is, to adopt a pragmatic approach, for this is the only way in which some progress towards the ethical goal can be made. Even the most moral politician has to master the type of prudential political calculus which is sometimes called the art of the possible, or his efforts will come to naught.

While there is in all political action a purely pragmatic ingredient—a consideration of available means under given conditions—it does not follow that the whole truth about politics was told by the author of *The Prince*. The art of the possible, if it is to be complete, must include considerations of a nonutilitarian, moral order. For an explication of that point we may rely on a philosopher and statesman with a keen appreciation of the Machiavellian aspect of politics, the Italian Benedetto Croce. Recognizing that "in political action, in attempts to reach a definite goal, everything becomes a political means—everything, including in certain respects morality and religion," Croce also warns against the belief that moral norms have no application to politics. Man, he argues, is a moral being as well as a utilitarian looking for success in his dealings. "It may not be imagined that there can exist a political man entirely devoid of moral conscience. This would be the same as admitting that a 'political man' can exist without being a 'man.'" [12] The human conscience does not abdicate in political affairs. Against the notion that there is one set of ethics for private life and another for public life, it cries out that "one cannot do evil in order to attain good, as though evil and good were merchandise to be exchanged; that our hands must be kept clean; that the quality of the means must not conflict with the quality of the end." [13] If it is true that moral conscience must by definition always be followed, it is also true that political necessity may in some difficult circumstances require extraordinary measures which break normally respected moral principles. This dilemma, Croce argues, is only apparent and based on a static, casuistic notion of morality. What is *necessary* to promote civilized order

---

12 Benedetto Croce, *Politics and Morals*, trans. Salvatore J. Castiglione (New York: Philosophical Library, 1945), 22, 25.

13 *Ibid.*, 3. It should be mentioned that from Croce's early political philosophy some inferences were drawn by others which have led some commentators to associate Croce, at least marginally, with the rise of Italian Fascism. While he does not escape all of the blame for these inferences, his political philosophy as a whole does not support this interpretation but makes it quite understandable that Croce, at considerable risk to himself, would become a public critic of the Fascist regime.

is also demanded by conscience, conventional moral standards notwithstanding. In the particular circumstances, the extraordinary means are in conformity with the moral end. Croce's argument is not that the end justifies the means—he flatly rejects this formula. His point is that as the goal is good, so are the means. The means in question are the only ones that can promote the good in the given situation, which is to say that they are moral. Politics has its own law of utility and convenience, but it is not a closed-off, self-sufficient sphere of activity. Utilitarian skill in attaining ends is a virtue in a politician, but he must never fail to take into account that men have a moral nature to which the pragmatic calculus must be adjusted.

The true statesman, we may conclude, has a clear conception of the moral end of human existence, and he will always strive to make politics subservient to that end. He is also sufficiently a realist to know that morality, in the strict sense of performing good acts for their own sake, will never become the law of politics. Even Plato reluctantly conceded that fact. We may infer that Jesus had the same in mind when he separated between the things of God and the things of Caesar. The statesman knows that the best he can normally hope for is to put self-interest in the service of moral ends. He can find some comfort in the fact that in most cases enlightened self-interest drives man in the direction of morality. As an example we may point to constitutionalism. The latter unquestionably owes much to sophisticated egotism. From a purely selfish point of view it is better to have rule of law than arbitrary government. [14] But constitutionalism also serves an ethical need. It is the political condition for the furtherance of the ethical life.

14 *Cf.* James M. Buchanan and Gordon Tullock, *The Calculus of Consent: Logical Foundations of Constitutional Democracy* (Ann Arbor: University of Michigan Press, 1962).

Lest the influence of ethical motives in politics be entirely discounted, it should also be noted that in a society where men are growing insensitive to the demands of the ethical life, their enlightened self-interest, too, will be increasingly difficult to discern. As their ethical vision is blurred, there is less to restrain their cruder inclinations. Men will become more indiscriminate in their choice of ends and means. The power struggle, which before was leavened somewhat by the ethical pull, will get harsher. Whereas ethical conscience, the will to the common good, used to give to the constitution and the laws generally an aura of dignity which made it easier for the citizens to recognize allegiance to the lawful order as being in their long-term interest, they are now going to look at the laws with less reverence and not be as predisposed against breaking them, if it would serve their own immediate goals and go undetected. In that sense, it may be said that any civilized political order is ultimately rooted in ethical conscience.

It should be evident from these remarks that the proposed attempt to give an ethical interpretation of democracy will not rest on some exaggerated view of the influence of moral motives in politics. It is clearly understood that politics has the dimension of conflict which is emphasized by many modern thinkers. The fact that references to moral principle are frequently on the lips of politicians is anything but a sure sign that they are propelled by moral considerations. One need not be a cynic to see that self-interest often masquerades in moral garb. At the same time, the need that the politician feels to give a moral justification for his proposals suggests a recognition that his potential supporters would like to feel that the policies they endorse are sanctioned by a higher court than the selfish ego. Why all these moral appeals in politics, now and throughout history, if there is not at the bottom of men's endless arguments about the proper political order also some-

thing more than a concern for private advantage, a real ethical awareness, however vague, that we may not proceed
arbitrarily? Whether the moral sentiments expressed by
politicians are for the most part genuinely felt or not, they indicate that there is more to politics than the power play, be it
crude and violent or modified by enlightened self-interest.

This study is an attempt to supply in broad outline what is
lacking in a theory of democracy which does not look beyond
the clash of wills. The needs of the ethical life cannot be ignored in a society which wants to be known as civilized. They
remain an unconditional demand on man, a constant reminder that a political order based on mere selfishness is not
worthy of man's true purpose. It is incumbent on the political
thinker to come to grips with the role of the ethical in human
affairs and try to answer the question of how it may be maintained and expanded in political life. The present study seeks
to perform that task in regard to democracy.

Human Experience and the "Scientific Method"

The development of an ethical theory of democracy comes up against a number of modern preconceptions about what type of evidence may be accepted by the political scientist. As has already been stated, conscience will be regarded here as an opening to the transcendent purpose of human life. This understanding of conscience forms part of a general view of human nature, according to which man has a spiritual existence, a kind of self-awareness and freedom that is lacking in physical nature and in the animal world. Together with the type of ethical philosophy with which it is indissolubly bound up, that view has come under attack as based on "unscientific," nonempirical evidence.

The last two centuries have seen a vast and increasing amount of activity in the natural sciences. The resulting progress in bringing physical nature under our control has endowed the methods of experimental science with an immense prestige, creating a wish in many quarters for their widest possible application. They have come to be viewed by some as the key to more complete and reliable knowledge, not only of inanimate nature, but of human nature and social life. The distinction between a specifically human, spiritual order, where freedom and responsibility are not only meaningful but unavoidable concepts, and a postulated "quantita-

27

tive" order of causal relationships has become blurred. Reflecting this general trend, modern political science is marked by a certain reluctance to study politics in the light of a philosophical understanding of man, one which views life from the perspective of actual human self-experience rather than in analogy with what is known pragmatically about physical nature. Many political scientists are prone to evade the difficult question of the special nature of man and its implications for the study of politics and proceed instead according to some version of the acclaimed "scientific method."

It is not possible here to state fully the case against making empirico-quantitative methods—and theory, viewed as a set of working hypotheses potentially capable of verification by such methods—the scientific norm for the study of political man. Just enough should be said to show that this approach suffers from grave difficulties. The following attempt to lift the ban on a certain type of evidence and reasoning will have the additional purpose of making the notion of a distinctively human, spiritual nature clearer. It should be noted that I shall be criticizing a *tendency* in modern political science (and other social sciences) rather than individual intellectual positions, such as may be found among those loosely and often ambiguously described as behavioralists. I am not trying to deny that there are political scientists sometimes said to be in the latter category who, especially in practice, go beyond a dogmatic adherence to empirico-quantitative methods and related types of theory. Needless to say, my argument is not directed against a general concern with finding support in facts for hypotheses. It is difficult to quarrel with the wish to acquire as much knowledge as possible about a subject, provided the subject is not trivial and the collection of information is guided by a sense of proportion. My criticism focuses on the tendency to define "facts" in sociopolitical matters with reference to what is so defined in the natural sciences, to assume, in other words, that the nature of man and society does not, in any way essential to a meaningful and reliable understanding of politics, transcend the type of reality which is postulated by the natural sciences. Although often mixed with or counterbalanced by less questionable approaches, this inclination remains a considerable influence. To the extent that social scientists exhibit this tendency, my argument applies; to the extent that they are beginning to question it, it is a reminder of sins past.

In the attempt to achieve the closest possible approximation to the principles of natural science in the study of politics, a premium is put on evidence believed to be quantitative or susceptible of quantification. According to one of the pioneers of this modern orientation, Arthur Bentley, the statement of social fact that "takes us farthest along the road toward quantitative estimates will inevitably be the best statement." In Bentley's view, "ideas" and "feelings" are not intelligible social forces but meaningless abstractions. The social scientist should try to eliminate such "unmeasurable elements" from his investigation and aim for the enviable position of the natural scientist whose research material is "susceptible of measurement and quantitative comparison all the way through." [1] One is reminded of William James's phrase that "you must bring out of each word its practical cash-value." [2] A more recent but very similar view of political science is that of David Easton. Although less hostile to "introspective psychology," Easton emphasizes the great indebtedness of the discipline to Bentley. Easton calls for the development of a theoretical "master plan" to guide empirical

1 Arthur F. Bentley, *The Process of Government* (Bloomington: Principia Press, 1935), 201, 200.
2 William James, *Essays in Pragmatism*, ed. Alburey Castell (New York: Hafner Publishing Co., 1968), 145.

research, which might one day conceivably "reach the stage of maturity associated with theory in physics, for example." Discussing his hopes for the discipline, he regrets that the physical sciences are centuries ahead of the social sciences and that therefore "all social research cannot yet be conducted with the methodological rigor familiar to the natural sciences or in terms of the systematic frameworks resembling the model of physics." [3]

In part, the attempted introduction into political science of methods believed to approach the type of rigor and precision characteristic of methods in the natural sciences may be a reaction against instances of sloppy scholarship and extravagant speculation in the past. But the proposed cure has important features which are as problematical as the disease. While it should not be denied that there are political investigations for which measurability in some sense of that word is a desirable goal, it can hardly be maintained that it should be sought even at the price of a one-sided or distorted view of political reality, not to mention triviality in the resulting findings. We would seem to be better advised to heed Aristotle's dictum that "it is the mark of an educated man to look for precision in each class of things just so far as the nature of the subjects admits." [4] Even more to the point, it can be argued that there is a type of philosophical exactitude or precision which has a better claim to those terms than any quantitative equivalent.

One of the stated purposes of using the scientific method in political science is to discover "patterns" or "uniformities" in political behavior. In the phrasing of a sympathetic explication of the method, "We . . . are assuming that these reg-

3 David Easton, *The Political System* (New York: Alfred A. Knopf, 1971), 177, 61, 58, 59.
4 Aristotle, *The Nicomachean Ethics*, trans. David Ross (London: Oxford University Press, 1954), 3 (1094b).

ularities can be expressed in generalizations which approximate the universality of a scientific law or theory in the natural sciences."[5] Presumably, this must be taken to mean that the special nature and complexity of human life is discounted or denied by political science proper. Or to state the same conclusion in a way that clarifies the word *special*: to the extent that important differences are recognized between man and thing and between man and animal, they are not believed to be of the order that different principles of explanation must be applied to each. It is hard to see that truth could be served by such a blurring of distinctions. To take an example, it is only by a facile reductionism that one can regard the effect of men's social background on their political actions as belonging to the same general category of "regularities" as the effect of one lever on another or the effect of some stimulus on a rat. It belongs to the specifically human sphere of conscious, purposive action. It has to be understood from within that context by methods which recognize the fundamental difference in meaning between the word *effect* as applied to human political behavior and the same word as applied to a piece of machinery or a biological organism.

The presumption in favor of applying the methods of natural science, as conceived by their proponents in the social sciences, to a political subject matter carries more far-reaching implications than is generally recognized. It is sometimes argued by advocates of the scientific method that its application to sociopolitical reality is not necessarily the equivalent of introducing a whole world view. It is said to be merely an attempt to pursue further a method which has been found to "work," in the sense, for instance, that it facilitates prediction. It must be asked, however, whether the effort to imitate

5 M. Margaret Conway and Frank B. Feigert, *Political Analysis: An Introduction* (Boston: Allyn & Bacon, 1972), 14.

natural science does not imply that human behavior is of a certain kind. If man as a political being transcends biology and physics in ways essential to the very definition of political life, exclusive employment of empirico-quantitative methods and related types of theory is unsatisfactory or misdirected. Their exclusive use in political science could be defended only if the "patterns" and "regularities" discernible in political life did *not* transcend the causal order of reality postulated by the natural sciences. The conclusion seems inescapable: if the scientific method is set up as the only way of acquiring reliable knowledge of sociopolitical reality, the latter is by that token assumed to conform in respect to its defining attributes to what we assume about the nature of relationships between phenomena in the physical and biological world. But in that case, a certain view of human nature and society is indeed tacitly presupposed.

It may be argued in response that it is only by concentrating on measurable phenomena and aiming for quantification that we can reach any exact and therefore meaningful knowledge of sociopolitical reality. But whence this presumption in favor of knowledge which is "exact" in the quantitative sense? If it has not somehow been determined beforehand what sociopolitical reality is like, why is it that only such knowledge is supposed to be meaningful?

The hidden hypothesis about man and society is always verified, or at least never contradicted, for all the "regularities" of political behavior are forced into the Procrustean bed of "scientific" explanation. It is assumed that the lingering element of uncertainty and unpredictability is either inaccessible by scholarly means or a merely temporary problem whose resolution will have to await more extensive research and further refinement of the methods. An almost Newtonian conception of reality often appears to be implied, one which has been found wanting even in physics. The humanistic-philosophic objection that the "patterns" of social life do not belong to the same category as "patterns" in astronomy or physics, for example, but are acts of will in a context of freedom, purpose, and responsibility is an objection which cannot be handled on its own ground. It must either be thrown out as "unscientific," and thus unworthy of scholarly consideration, or emasculated through a redefinition of the concepts used in terms of the scientific method, that is, by a reduction of them to a predetermined level of explanation.

The point to be made is that the proponents of an exclusive or primary reliance on empirico-quantitative methods in political science are exhibiting a fundamental arbitrariness in their determination of scientific relevance. It becomes the more glaring if the need for a philosophical understanding of human nature and society is simultaneously discounted. It is difficult to see how one could defend setting up the methods of natural science or some approximation thereof as the ideal for social science before it has been determined through some kind of assessment of human nature in its complex wholeness to what extent these criteria can be applied to the study of man in the first place. These are philosophical questions, and very difficult questions at that. In order to understand the role and meaning of politics in human life and what methods are appropriate to that task, it is necessary to engage in a type of investigation in which the facts of actual human self-experience are allowed to speak for themselves. It will not do for the political scientist to begin by introducing an inflexible rule of evidence borrowed from a specialized branch of research. To deny the primacy of a philosophical grasp of human nature while insisting on the universal applicability of the scientific method is tantamount to setting up that method as the final judge of reality and thus to adopt a rigid metaphysical system. To admit the need for philosophy, in the sense of a scientifically valid examination of experience, is to have left the confines of empirico-quantitative methods, for philosophical reasoning is not an application of those methods or related types of theory, but a comprehensive assessment of reality logically prior to them.

The present argument in favor of philosophy is not intended to deny that it has been found highly useful for certain purposes to proceed as though man were a mere part of the physical universe postulated by natural science. The latter approach has allowed man to exercise a particular type of control over his destiny. To take just a single example, the concept of cause and effect has proved very helpful in the development of such fields as physics. To recognize the pragmatic value of this and other concepts of natural science is not the same as adopting the "scientistic" view of the world. The latter is based on the elevation of the physical universe from the status of an abstract hypothetical construct, useful in some fields of inquiry, to the status of reality itself. This is simply to ignore the whole body of humanistic evidence available to philosophy: man as known by us in actual experience is not locked into some vast, causally determined system. To be human is to be engaged in conscious, purposeful activity, to reflect about and choose between alternative lines of conduct. We know ourselves to be interfering to some extent with the flow of events, shaping it according to our own intentions. Our direct knowledge of freedom in the moment of choice is an emphatic, indeed final, humanistic refutation of the allegation that human behavior may be explained in analogy with, for instance, some balls on a billiard table knocking against each other and the walls of the table. Mechanistic theories of human nature may perhaps have a certain coherence when considered in the abstract, but as interpretations of the concrete reality known to the living, acting human being, they are wholly inappropriate.

The language of philosophical self-interpretation consists of concepts like "experience," "act," "intend," and "freedom." These are indispensable in an analysis of specifically human life, but become meaningless if applied to things. Things do not "experience," "act," "intend," etc. Conversely, the language of "cause and effect," "function," etc., used in the physical sciences, is alien to the mode of distinctively human activity, although sometimes used metaphorically to describe it. The theory that freedom is but an unscientific illusion to be progressively dispelled by the discovery of causal "patterns" in different areas of research remains a metaphysical allegation, an abstract afterthought doing violence to an immediate awareness. By an illegitimate and arbitrary inference from tentative intellectual constructs developed by the experimental sciences a confining and distorting explanatory scheme is clamped on actual human experience.

Political research allegedly conducted according to the scientific method is usually saved by the constant and unavoidable intrusion of humanistic interpretations. These recapture for the researcher himself and the student of his findings some of the humanistic meaning which is lost through the attempted methodological reduction of political reality. One may indeed question whether the proponents of strict adherence to the scientific method ever come very close to their stated ideal for the discipline. I have been arguing, therefore, not primarily against what these political scientists are actually doing, although there is considerable room for criticism in this area, but against what they are *attempting* to do.

Although anything but dead, the "scientistic" temptation does not appear quite as strong in political science as it once

was. This may well be a sign of a beginning rediscovery of
the specifically human order of activity. Perhaps there is
then also hope for the recovery of a humanistic, philosophical science of politics for which concepts like *freedom* and
purpose are not unwelcome complications but a challenge to
reflection.

Self-Awareness

The physicist and the chemist have a great deal to tell us
about man. So does the biologist. It has not been my intention
to deny that in a manner of speaking man resembles the animal. He has needs which may be viewed as growing out of
his participation in the organic world. But the empirical concepts of natural science do not speak with precision about
the universal, permanent structure of experience, as does
philosophy, but are hypothetical, pragmatic constructs always subject to revision. What is of first importance to the
political scientist is that, except for specific limited purposes,
man cannot be treated only empirically as an organism with
needs that are understood in the corresponding fashion. Man
is, to use Ernst Cassirer's phrase, the *animal symbolicum*, the
being with an intelligence and imagination which works
through symbols.[6] The human mind, Susanne Langer argues, is "an organ in the service of primary needs, but of
characteristically human needs."[7] Whatever the likenesses between man and animal, the pervasiveness of symbolization in
human thought establishes one all-important difference.
That difference, which has a direct bearing on the study of
politics, has been extensively investigated by an important

6 See Ernst Cassirer, *An Essay on Man* (New Haven: Yale University Press,
  1962).
7 Susanne K. Langer, *Philosophy in a New Key* (New York: New American Library, 1951), 43 (emphasis in original).

school of modern research, often called "philosophical anthropology," which has drawn on and integrated findings from biology, zoology, animal psychology, anthropology, and philosophy. Cassirer and Langer are two leading contributors known primarily as philosophers. [8]

Research in this area continues, and it is of course possible that the views of the philosophical anthropologists regarding the difference between man and animal will require some modification in the future. My general argument is not dependent, however, on the precision with which they have distinguished between the two. Even if it were established, for instance, that some animals have more of a symbolical grasp than is recognized by the philosophical anthropologists, their understanding of human nature would still be intact. It would simply mean that some animals have more in common with humans than previously thought, and that the methods of animal psychology would have to be adjusted accordingly.

Philosophical anthropology has argued that what makes man distinctively human is a unique kind of self-awareness which is made possible by symbolical thought. Whereas the animal appears to have only the perspective on the world which inheres in its practical need of the moment, man has the ability to step outside of himself, as it were, and look at phenomena, including himself, from an unlimited number of angles. He can detach himself from his locus in time and place by the use of symbols. Man seems to be the only crea-

8 The following discussion of the difference between man and animal makes use in a very summary fashion of arguments that are presented in detail in the following works: Cassirer, *An Essay on Man*; Langer, *Philosophy in a New Key*; Max Scheler, *Man's Place in Nature*, trans. Hans Meyerhoff (Boston: Beacon Press, 1961); Arnold Gehlen, *Anthropologische Forschung* (Hamburg: Rowohlt, 1961); Adolf Portmann, *Zoologie und das neue Bild des Menschen* (Hamburg: Rowohlt, 1956); F. J. J. Buytendijk, *Mensch und Tier* (Hamburg: Rowohlt, 1958); J. v. Uexküll and G. Kriszat, *Streifzüge durch die Umwelten von Tieren und Menschen: Bedeutungslehre* (Hamburg: Rowohlt, 1956).

ture who can form the idea of a "thing" in the sense of a distinct and permanent event. That requires a mind which en-
dows perceptions with complex and enduring meanings. In
man, any number of images may enter symbolically into the
perception of an orange, so that we are not only aware of
what is immediately present to the senses, its shape or color,
but can also "see" its extension in space, its softness, juici-
ness, taste, possible uses, etc. Symbolization allows the mind
to play around phenomena, to fit them into contexts of the
past, present, and future. To the animal, objects do not seem
to have this quality of being separate and permanent entities
in a wider world, but instead receive their content from a
present need. For the hungry dog a bone is "something to
eat," for the playful dog "something to play with." Whatever
it is depends on the desire of the moment. It can not be imagined apart from an immediate urge.

What is sometimes called animal language consists, not of
symbols, which denote meanings detached from a present
perception, but of *signs*—a bark, growl, or the like, triggered
by what is in the animal's awareness at the moment, as for
example, a hostile gesture in another animal. Susanne
Langer argues that the mind of even a very clever dog is "a
simple and direct *transmitter* of messages from the world to
his motor centers." [9] Animal "language" is not symbolical, but
symptomatic. Aristotle was getting at the same difference
when he said that "speech is something different from
voice." [10]

The point is not that animals lack intelligence of every
kind. If by that word is meant "either adjustment to the immediate environment or adaptive modification of environ-

9 Langer, *Philosophy in a New Key*, 37.
10 Aristotle, *The Politics*, trans. T. A. Sinclair (Harmondsworth: Penguin Books,
   1962), 28.

ment,"[11] many animals must be said to possess it to a high degree. The point is that the animal lacks, or has just the barest rudiments of, a type of intelligence and imagination which involves detachment from the here and now.

In man, all experience automatically undergoes what Susanne Langer calls "symbolic transformation."[12] The stream of perception and impulse is broken up and transformed. Its content is spread out before the eyes of the mind in symbolical form. Man is not immersed in his own impulses, but has a perspective on them. Whether he wants it or not, he is presented with an opportunity to analyze and evaluate them. He is not caught in some chain of stimulus and response. In Cassirer's words: "There is an unmistakable difference between organic reactions and human responses. In the first case a direct and immediate answer is given to an outward stimulus; in the second case the answer is delayed. It is interrupted and retarded by a slow and complicated process of thought."[13] Reinhold Niebuhr speaks of a specifically human "consciousness of consciousness" or "self-transcendence" which "expresses itself in terms of memory and foresight."[14] In the inner monologue which is characteristic of man, present perceptions, memories, and projections are freely manipulated to fit whatever purpose he has in mind. Whereas the animal seems forever bound to its peculiar pattern of behavior, man can imagine himself in new circumstances.

The human being is aware of himself as a part of a greater whole. He has a world. He is capable of a structured view of reality. He can study his environment scientifically, and he can build imaginary worlds. To be human is to be creative.

11 Cassirer, An Essay on Man, 33.
12 Langer, Philosophy in a New Key, 33–54, passim.
13 Cassirer, An Essay on Man, 24.
14 Reinhold Niebuhr, The Nature and Destiny of Man (2 vols.; New York: Charles Scribner's Sons, 1964), I, 72; see also 68–74, passim.

Where there is human life, there is culture. The process of symbolization which underlies this activity is an essential part of what I have called man's spirituality. Max Scheler writes: "The spiritual being . . . is no longer subject to its drives and its environment. Instead, it is 'free from the environment' or . . . 'open to the world.'"[15] The same aspect of man's spiritual nature is described by Paul Tillich: "Man has a world, namely a structured whole of innumerable parts, a *cosmos*, as the Greeks called it, because of its structured character which makes it accessible to men through acts of creative receiving and transforming. Having a world is more than having an environment."[16]

Symbolization makes man free in a sense in which the animal is not. It also presents him with a unique problem. How is he to guide his actions? The animal is deeply sunk in instincts that help direct its behavior. It is secure in inherited natural drives that fit it into the environment. Since man's self-awareness is constituted by a certain detachment from his own drives, it is highly questionable to talk about instincts in a human context. In man, Arnold Gehlen points out, the steady, stereotyped instinctual patterns found in the animal have been torn down. At the most, humans may be said to have "instinctual residues." They are "instinctually insecure." They must look elsewhere for guidance.[17]

Like the animal, man is full of impulses and desires. But they do not automatically result in action. They are absorbed into the human inner monologue where they are mingled with other impulses. Symbolization transforms everything into infinitely complex combinations. In the medium of

15 Scheler, *Man's Place in Nature*, 37.
16 Paul Tillich, *Morality and Beyond* (New York: Harper & Row, 1963), 19.
17 These phrases are used by Gehlen in *Anthropologische Forschung*, where he also shows that in man culture has taken the place of instinct.

human consciousness it becomes impossible to distinguish clearly this drive from that. To take just one example, it is not possible to separate the sexual urge in man from such other influences as a will to power, a sense of beauty, or a wish to procreate. There are in man no ready-made guides to action, and it is not possible to sink back into instinct. The unique type of self-awareness which is engendered by symbolical thought makes man subject to the vagaries of his own imagination.

The specifically human way of structuring life is for man to impose rules on himself. For "instinctually insecure" man, as opposed to the animal, it is necessary to *create* patterns of behavior. Out of this need for self-discipline, dictated by his special nature, grow the norms of culture. These are not the result of blind spontaneity, but of conscious intent to escape the chaos which is always possible in the *animal symbolicum*.

The findings of the philosophical anthropologists support the old Greek notion that man is by nature a social being. Social life begins with man's ability to step outside of his here and now. Because he is not bound to any one perspective on himself and his environment, but can enter imaginatively into any number of points of view, he can put himself in the place of others and share meanings with them. Symbolical thought forms the basis for all kinds of cooperation and organization. It is the necessary prerequisite for grasping the idea of a role, and thus the idea of a society. As the *animal symbolicum*, man can think of himself as playing a part in a larger scheme and can thus have a conception of politics, constitutions, and other laws. Contrary to what is the case among animals, humans have an elaborate social awareness. The difference between herd instinct and social consciousness is not one of degree but of kind. It makes little sense to talk, as does Maurice Duverger, for instance, of "animal societies" with "politics," "authority," and "organized power." [18] These terms have real meaning only in a human context, that is, a context of symbolical activity. They can be made to fit animal behavior only after they have been redefined to the point of almost complete removal of their original human content. As John Dewey points out, "no amount of aggregate collective action of itself constitutes a community." [19]

The Human Frame of Reference

For the political scientist to adjust his methods to the spiritual reality of human self-awareness and the type of freedom it involves represents a great improvement over the attempt to reduce man for purposes of scientific explanation to a common level with biological organisms or physical things. But neither can man be regarded as a mere economical creature, a skillful organizer with an ability to calculate how best to satisfy his desires now and in the future, as some political scientists would seem to contend or imply. [20] Symbolical activity permits the discovery of enlightened self-interest, but it also makes possible the entertainment of ethical ideals. It permits man to evaluate himself morally by enabling him to contrast his present state with an image of what his life should really be like.

If anything stands out in the history of culture, it is that man has used his ability to think in symbols to express his sense of moral right and his sense of the divine. Man is an

18 Maurice Duverger, *The Idea of Politics* (London: Methuen & Co., 1966), 6–12, *passim*.
19 John Dewey, *The Public and Its Problems* (Chicago: Swallow Press, 1954), 151.
20 For examples of reasoning that goes in that direction see Anthony Downs, *An Economic Interpretation of Democracy* (New York: Harper & Bros., 1957), and William Riker, *The Theory of Political Coalitions* (New Haven: Yale University Press, 1962).

ethical and religious being with corresponding needs. Many will deny that there is a moral absolute or a God. That does not change the fact that man is forever struggling with the ethical question of right and with the religious question of man's relation to the divine. To be human is to have these concerns. They will not go away just because from time to time they are pronounced irrational or meaningless. One may even doubt that they cease to bother those who claim to regard them in that way. It appears to be human nature to break out of such attempts to restrict the process of self-interpretation characteristic of man.

It should be sufficiently clear from the above arguments that what is specifically human about man, a certain kind of self-consciousness involving a trans-subjective sharing of meaning and with an ethical and religious dimension, is not accessible by the same kinds of methods which are used to investigate physical things or organisms. Inasmuch as man's spiritual nature is the very mode of social life, empirico-quantitative methods, understood as an approximation of the principles of natural science, will serve the social scientist poorly. What is needed is a humanistic approach, one which puts a premium on familiarity with and respect for the facts of the living reality of distinctively human behavior. As has already been argued in different ways, human action must be examined "from within," that is, from within immediate experience of life in the concrete.

That does not mean that what is loosely called "empirical facts" can be ignored. Much information which is so labeled provides indispensable knowledge about political man. What should not be forgotten, however, is that the nature and importance of "facts" can be known only in the light of a philosophical understanding of human nature which deals with human meanings on their own ground. Drawing on our discussion about the symbolical character of consciousness, we can see that the term *empirical fact* is a highly ambiguous one. In sociopolitical life, what is such a fact? The word *empirical* is usually taken to refer to phenomena which are perceived by the senses. According to Frank Sorauf, political science is "committed to the proposition that knowledge of social behavior and institutions must come from experience, from sense perception of events in the real world." [21] Such a view of the source of knowledge reveals a basic vagueness. To the extent that man is aware of phenomena, they have already been taken up in the medium of symbolical thought. That means that they have been endowed with complex meanings. The fact that an impression is received through the senses, whatever that means, does not make the phenomenon present itself to man in no uncertain terms. As a part of human consciousness it is fitted into and understood through a complicated pattern of preconceptions, memories, taboos, ideals, and prejudices. A so-called empirical fact is pregnant with symbolical content. Far from being self-evident with respect to its own reality, it has to be deciphered. Only after philosophical reason has determined the nature of the "fact," that is, its place in the vast conceptual structure which constitutes man's knowledge of reality, is it possible to know by what method it should be investigated. Empirical political reality turns out to be much more complex and unpredictable than is allowed for by the scientific method.

The theory of democracy that I wish to present will view government as part of a specifically human order of activity with a definite ethical end. It draws on what may be called humanistic evidence, facts about man illuminated by philosophical self-knowledge. As already hinted, that does

21 Frank J. Sorauf, *Perspectives on Political Science* (Columbus: Charles E. Merrill Books, 1965), 22.

not mean that the scholar is thrown back on subjective experience. Consciousness has a dimension of universality. The process of symbolization which pervades human experience makes few meanings radically inaccessible to men in general. The individual can transmit his own perceptions of life to others and make the perceptions of others his own. Art in its various forms is just one example. Social life must indeed be regarded as a trans-subjective existence. It is doubtful that one can really distinguish what in one's knowledge of the human condition comes out of one's own experience and what has been contributed by others. "Private" and "social" are inextricably related. Paradoxically, self-discovery is a communal, cultural process. It will be argued in particular later that the pursuit of the ethical life is a supra-individual task. Evidence about ethical conscience is available from all of those who have taken its normative authority seriously and tried to determine its role in the structure of human existence. Self-knowledge is a dialectical process in which the testimony of many, reflected in part in the cultural traditions of mankind, is tested against immediate experience, which is itself largely dependent on that testimony.

To offer an ethical interpretation of democracy is to appeal to the universal element in moral experience. Unless men have, potentially at least, a common frame of reference grounded in reality itself, arguments about the human condition could never convince, but only flatter. To speak of moral experience as inherently and exclusively subjective is to rule out agreement on what is good or bad. An apparent overlapping of individual preferences in some particular case does not by itself constitute moral agreement, for it need not involve a shared understanding of the essential meaning and purpose of human life. Needless to say, men are likely always to have some differences of opinion regarding the precise nature of ethical conscience, but arguments about it assume that there are interpretations which come closer to the truth than others.

Many today deny that there is a commonality of moral experience. They maintain that arguments about the normative validity of ethical judgments are scientifically pointless. To the extent that this view grows out of an appreciation of the uniqueness of individual circumstances, it proceeds from an observation not wholly incompatible with the ethical theory I am presenting. Missing in the various doctrines of subjectivism, however, is the crucial recognition that although no two situations are exactly the same they are subject to the same moral imperative. Morality is a synthesis between universal and individual. The content of particular moral acts varies with the circumstances to which they are adjusted, but the inspiration and purpose remain the same. Philosophy seeks to describe how the moral synthesis is achieved. It interprets a type of experience which transcends the subjective.

It is contended that as social scientists we must keep "facts" and "values" separate. It is not possible to give a full-fledged refutation of this attempted dichotomy in these pages. But criticism of it has been implied and will be implied in the following chapters, to the effect that the "fact-value" distinction becomes plausible only in conjunction with the questionable assumption that a "fact" is some sort of static and independently existing phenomenon. My own analysis indicates that "facts" have to be understood as integral parts of, and means in, the effort to achieve a comprehensive grasp of reality. The symbols which give them meaning set them in this wider context and are thus reminders of the totality to which they belong. That totality emerges out of man's conceptual structuring of concrete experience. But experience is already guided by and understood through this continuous process of interpretation, so that theory and practice, intellectual and moral activity, are developing together in a dialectical fashion. They are indissolubly intertwined, as is thought with its substance. All human action is at the same time valuation. Factual, conceptual statements about it thus express a moral reality. To try to extract from a "fact" its "value" component is only to conceal from view that what is designated a "fact" is simultaneously and unavoidably assigned a positive or negative role in the achievement of the comprehensive goal whose value is necessarily affirmed whenever the designating activity is performed.

Our way of interpreting reality, our sense of proportion and value, is the result of innumerable acts of will and related conceptual adjustments in the past. "Thus, in the sciences of man . . . there can be a valid response to 'I don't understand' which takes the form, not only 'develop your intuitions,' but more radically 'change yourself.' This puts an end to any aspiration to a value-free . . . science of man. A study of man is inseparable from an examination of the options between which men must choose." Such an examination requires not only an intellectual absorption of abstract ideas, but an orientation of the whole personality which connects the symbols with experience. Obviously, intelligent choice presupposes a standard: "The superiority of one position over another will . . . consist in this, that from the more adequate position one can understand one's own stand and that of one's opponent, but not the other way around. It goes without saying that this argument can only have weight for those in the superior position." [22] Far from indicating moral or intellectual arrogance, this statement, which expresses an

22 Charles Taylor, "Interpretation and the Sciences of Man," *Review of Metaphysics*, XXV (September, 1971), 47–48. For other arguments against the "fact-vaule" dichotomy see Leo Strauss, *Natural Right and History* (Chicago: University of Chicago Press, 1953), especially Chap. 2; and Eric Voegelin, *The New Science of Politics* (Chicago: University of Chicago Press, 1952), especially the introduction.

ancient and fundamental insight, simply points out that a view of reality is superior to another by virtue of its conceptual comprehensiveness. The quoted passages emphasize the close relationship between ethical and intellectual activity and raise the question whether those who embrace the "fact-value" distinction are doing so because in the given sense they have mastered the opposing older view, inspired by the classical and Judaeo-Christian experience, and found it wanting, or because they have failed to master it.

Philosophical scholarship aims at the most complete understanding of reality. The modern attempt to separate "facts" and "values" and the related tendency to accept only so-called "empirical facts" as a source of reliable knowledge, we may venture to say, represent a contraction in the interpretation of experience. The proper remedy for extravagant claims and premature certainty in moral matters is not a refusal to inquire into the validity of statements about the good for man, but a more scrupulous analysis of moral experience as it relates to various aspects of life.

To those who embrace the dominant modern view, the notion of an ethical interpretation of democracy will seem subjectivistic and presumptuous. "Who is to say what is moral?" But is it really presumptuous to suggest that arguments about man's ethical life can be tested against objective reality, to submit that our feelings of moral obligation are not just impenetrable enigmas of subjectivity, but have a trans-subjective, trans-temporal origin and focus which can be illuminated by philosophy? Since perfect and total knowledge can safely be ruled out, this view does not imply an eventual cessation of argument. The belief that an objective principle of morality exists does not end, but gives rise to inquiry. In point of fact, is it not less presumptuous to say that the good for man is a matter about which we may profitably argue, than to refuse to entertain the idea that reliable knowledge in this area is possible? The latter attitude, although allegedly expressive of intellectual humility, would actually seem to have in it a considerable measure of dogmatism and arrogance. An attempt to interpret democracy in the light of a serious consideration of man's sense of higher destiny, we may at least hope, should help to diminish rather than increase the threat of intellectual capriciousness. It places a central part of human experience and its relation to basic problems of politics under the purview of critical examination.

The next step in this development of an ethical interpretation of democracy will be to try to discern the general form taken by ethical awareness and activity. In what way does man grasp and affirm his transcendent goal? Since the intrinsic worth of the structuring influence of ethical conscience is here assumed, such a "formal" approach is at the same time necessarily a study of the substantive content of morality. The argument is that ethical conscience is experienced as a restraint on impulse. That is another way of saying that a certain type of self-restraint has moral worth. Having analyzed the process by which moral order is realized, we shall be looking for its implications for the organization of popular rule. This ethical philosophy will be clarified and related to the institutional questions of democracy through a careful examination of Rousseau's theory of popular government. Such an analysis will help to demonstrate the close relationship between ethics and politics and, more specifically, the serious moral difficulties with the concept of plebiscitary democracy. By way of elimination, the argument will proceed in the direction of a more tenable position and will conclude with a consideration of the concept of constitutional democracy. The purpose is not to develop some sort of moral "casuistry" of democracy and an elaborate set of institutional prescriptions. This investigation is best described as a search for the general principle for the reconciliation of the needs of the ethical life with popular self-rule. The important and very difficult task of applying this principle to the various practical problems of democracy will be only just begun.

PART TWO

The Ethical Life

The Duality of Human Nature

I have argued in a preliminary fashion that politics has a transcendent moral end and that a truly civilized society is possible only if the demands of the ethical life are recognized and respected. A treatment of the implications of that observation for democracy requires a more extensive explication of the ethical philosophy which is being advanced. More detailed answers must be given to these questions: what is the nature of the ultimate standard by which the quality of social and political life has to be judged and to which democracy, like other forms of government, must be adjusted? How does the structuring principle of man's ethical life order his actions? Before that principle is related to democracy, it also needs to be related to the more general ideas of community and culture.

Man's ethical conscience has been described earlier as a sense of sacred purpose. The latter term lends itself to a religious interpretation. For some Christians, I have said, it might seem preferable to speak of the guiding presence of the Holy Spirit. Although it is not the intention here to introduce a theological perspective, it is doubtful that man's ethical life as understood in the following discussion could be sharply distinguished from religion. Even if not bound up with a certain theology, a life centered in the recognition of a transcendent spiritual goal for man would appear to come very close to it. [1] Allegiance to an ethical end conceived as an ultimate of meaning and worth could involve a spiritual commitment similar to that which is ordinarily associated in the West with the worship of a personal God.

The view of the ethical life which will be developed here is deeply colored by the Christian tradition, but it also draws on the classical teaching of Plato and Aristotle, whose theology is quite different from that of Christianity. My purpose is to give an account of moral experience while staying short of theological claims about the nature of the divine reality in the direction of which man is ultimately pointed by ethical conscience. Ethical philosophy does not have to compete with theology. It leaves the possibility open of putting the elements of the ethical life in a broader context. It does not necessarily deny the claim that the facts of the ethical life take on additional significance when viewed from the privileged perspective of revelation. At the same time, if the structuring principle of man's ethical life is a manifestation of divine reality, it is evident that what philosophy can say about it has theological ramifications.

We are proceeding on the assumption that up to a certain point, which probably cannot be clearly defined, the ability to grasp the facts of man's ethical life is not dependent on accepting a particular theology. A Christian, a Buddhist, a Platonist, and an Aristotelian, for example, all recognize the presence in man of a transcendent spiritual awareness and a tension between that sense of higher destiny and contrary in-

---

1 Paul Tillich is prepared to use the word *faith* even about those who do not believe in transcendent reality, those he calls "humanists." Their lives may still center around an "ultimate concern," and "if faith is understood as the state of being ultimately concerned about the ultimate, humanism implies faith." Paul Tillich, *Dynamics of Faith* (New York: Harper & Bros., 1957), 62. My own theory implies a "faith" that does have a transcendent object.

clinations. Their differing theological views do not preclude
far-reaching agreement on the basic nature of man's moral
predicament.

But what about the person who claims to have no inkling of
a transcendent goal for man? Will he be without referents in
personal experience for the following account of the ethical
life? It should be stressed in response that the term ethical
conscience is not intended to signify some unique, specialized
reality revealed only to a privileged few. Its referent is so general, in fact, that it helps to define the human. To be sure,
some must have a less confused conception of it than others,
as is true of any subject; varying degrees of insight into the
nature of man are implied in the recognized need for
philosophical scholarship. While it cannot be ruled out
categorically that there are actually individuals who completely lack what I call ethical conscience, few would flatly
deny that they have any "conscience" at all. It is hard, if not
impossible, to imagine a human being who does not have his
moments of moral guilt, remorse, and reassurance. Many
will hasten to point out, however, that the "conscience" is of
course nothing but internalized social norms, merely a mask
for their own selfish interest, or the like. They will, in other
words, admit having a "conscience," a recurrent sense of
moral censure or approval, but attempt to explain away whatever moral authority it wields over them by introducing an
explanatory theory which rules out the possibility of objective
moral judgments.

To find referents in personal experience for our account of
the ethical life it is not necessary to abandon entirely the idea
that "conscience" in the loose, day-to-day sense of the word,
is a veil before subjective and possibly even blatantly selfish
intentions. It would be difficult to dispute that men's purported ethical motives are often mingled with, or even com-

pletely made up of, morally dubious content. Perspicacity regarding such subtle influences on human action must indeed be considered an asset in the ethical philosopher. It is necessary, however, that those who depreciate "conscience" make room for the possibility at least that what little moral authority it carries may be more than arbitrary. The facts of the ethical life must be allowed to stand without the restrictive interpretation put on them by dogmatic relativistic or nihilistic theory. This may be considered too much to ask, for such a concession would involve more than just a suspension of judgment. What is needed is indeed a measure of that ethical insight whose existence is the very subject of controversy.

But even among those who are generally sympathetic to the idea of a universal principle of good, certain habits of thought may stand in the way of grasping my concept of ethical conscience. It is quite common to think of "conscience" as a precarious guide to conduct. It becomes reliable, it is sometimes said, only to the extent that it can draw on a sound standard set apart from it. A Christian, for instance, may argue that "conscience" needs to be trained by Christian faith and that if it is not, it can lead man astray. It is also suggested that "conscience" may tell different individuals different things and that therefore an external criterion of judgment is needed to adjudicate moral disputes. This way of using the term is psychological and pragmatic rather than philosophical. I could only agree that man's moral judgments are aided by sound intellectual and moral training. It is an equally elementary observation that such judgments are likely to be colored by cultural and individual bias. The concept of ethical conscience I am setting forth here, however, refers to that element in moral experience which is *not* conditioned or transitory, but which *transcends* all bias. The concept signifies the ethical ultimate, the permanent, unvarying dimension of man's moral awareness. It would be an indication of not having grasped this concept to ask questions of this kind: "But don't men of conscience sometimes disagree about what is moral?" The answer is that ethical conscience, as I understand it, is never an "unreliable" or "precarious" guide to action. It always wills one and the same thing: the good. It is itself the final, "external" criterion. The element of precariousness in the moral life is introduced by man's inability or unwillingness fully to articulate his sense of spiritual purpose. By ethical conscience, then, I mean that higher intuition whose nature it is to pull man out of the cultural, denominational, or personal biases of mere "conscience." It is through ethical conscience that we become aware of moral imperfection. It is this transcendent power which leads man to seek the liberation from such limiting influences.

Central to the ethical philosophy that informs this study is the idea of the duality of human nature. Since the term *dualism* has been used by different philosophers in different ways, its meaning here needs to be delineated with considerable care. It goes almost without saying that I cannot hope to establish conclusively the validity of the concept of dualism which is being advanced. That would require lengthy philosophical arguments far beyond the scope of this investigation. What can and should be done is to present the concept with some thoroughness and to locate it roughly within the Western philosophical tradition.

It should perhaps be stated explicitly that the following exposition does not presume to be a distillation or summary of everything that is valid in the classical and Judaeo-Christian tradition in ethics. It has the much more limited purpose of developing a few selected themes emerging out of that tradition which are particularly relevant to our present investigation. The argument will prepare the ground specifically for analysis of Rousseau's view of ethics and politics and more generally for my concept of constitutionalism. The following discussion of some aspects of the duality of human nature will combine independent reflection with reliance on the ideas of other thinkers. The influence of Plato and Aristotle will be apparent. Much use will also be made of the thought of Irving Babbitt (1865–1933) and Paul Elmer More (1864–1937), two important American philosophers and literary critics. [2]

Whatever their differences on the theological level, the classical Greek philosophers and the leading Christian thinkers who together laid the foundation for the traditional Western view of man are at one in asserting that man is a creature of two worlds. He partakes of two intimately related and yet distinct orders of reality, one immanent and finite, one transcendent and infinite. For Plato, the central and most glaring fact of human existence is the paradox of the one and the many, the coexistence in life of unity and multiplicity, order and disorder. There is thrust on the philosopher the simultaneous awareness of a purpose of being, an end of meaning and worth, and of an opposing reality tending by its own nature towards nothingness. Perhaps the most persistent of all

2 Irving Babbitt taught most of his life at Harvard. He was a professor of French and comparative literature, but his works deal as much with philosophy and ethics. Paul Elmer More was partly an academician, teaching at Princeton, for instance, partly a literary journalist, in which capacity he was editor-in-chief of *The Nation*. His numerous philosophical and literary works include books on Plato. Together, Babbitt and More were the main source of intellectual inspiration for the cultural movement called the New Humanism, whose influence was most powerfully felt in the 1920s and 1930s. Among those who can be said to have belonged to it or absorbed many of its ideas are T. S. Eliot, Norman Foerster, Austin Warren, and Walter Lippmann.

This interpretation of Babbitt's and More's ideas owes much to Folke Leander's philosophical study, *The Inner Check: A Concept of Paul Elmer More with Reference to Benedetto Croce* (London: Edward Wright, 1974).

philosophical themes is summed up in these words: "Man is a strange mixture of being and non-being." [3] Human life is a perpetual and ever-changing flow of thoughts, impressions, feelings, and actions; yet amidst this endless variety and motion man is able to retain an image of human identity and perfection. He is not lost in a chaos of multiplicity. His world has a center which holds it together. There is in our consciousness, Irving Babbitt observes, "an element of oneness somewhere with which to measure the infinite otherwiseness of things." [4] Disorder is modified by the mysterious presence of a principle of order. In ethical terms this fundamental dualism of human existence can be defined as a tension between the universal good and all that thwarts its purpose in the world.

Before continuing, it should be made clear that the present discussion is concerned with the element of ethical order in life. We are interested in that aspect of the paradox of the one and the many which Plato himself regards as fundamental. While it is not necessary for the purpose of this study to explore at length the types of order that do not have a distinctively ethical origin, the existence of that complication must be remembered.

The paradox described here by the word *dualism* should be understood as prior to all theoretical undertakings, as the very starting point of philosophy. It is the primordial given of man's immediate awareness of reality. The paradox of dualism is the category in terms of which philosophy may attempt to describe reality but beyond which it cannot go, because it is itself constituted by it. The same thought is ex-

3 Ernst Cassirer, *An Essay on Man* (New Haven: Yale University Press, 1962), 11.
4 Irving Babbitt, *Democracy and Leadership* (New York: Houghton Mifflin Co., 1924), 9.

pressed somewhat differently by Irving Babbitt: "Life does
not give here an element of oneness and there an element of
change. It gives a *oneness that is always changing*. The oneness
and the change are inseparable." [5] Man does not somehow
fluctuate between the two poles of his being, living then in
the one, now in the other. To be human is to live in both at
once, to know order and disorder by each other. Order is
known as order in an immediate perception of reality. The
role of philosophy is to reflect upon and give conceptual form
to the content of this dualistic intuition.

The concept of dualism which is being developed needs to
be distinguished from other attempts to deal with the same
basic paradox. Few philosophers fail to recognize in some
form the tension within man's awareness of reality, but many
are led to interpret it in terms of a single principle which
supplants the paradox and denies its essential reality. The attempt to go beyond the dualism which is directly given in
human consciousness results either in a denial of transcendence, as in various naturalistic philosophies, or in a deifica-
tion of immanent reality, as in the case of Hegel. Hegel is
more sensitive than most to the dualism of being, but by trying to subsume it under the categories of an idealistic
monism, he comes close to denying the existential reality of
the tension which his dialectical logic is designed to comprehend.

The classical and Judaeo-Christian tradition has for the
most part resisted the temptation to resolve the paradox by
some such metaphysical means. As against naturalistic denials of a transcendent order of morality it has affirmed on
the basis of concrete human experience man's ability to know
that reality. As against attempts to identify man with the di-

5 Irving Babbitt, *Rousseau and Romanticism* (Cleveland: World Publishing Co.,
1964), 7.

vine it has insisted, likewise on the basis of concrete human experience, on the finitude of all human achievements.

My conception of dualism should not be mistaken for the distinction between body and soul which has played a considerable role in Western philosophy. The tension of concern here is that between the totality of finite human reality and the infinite demand placed on that reality by ethical conscience. To the realm of the finite belong not only our "bodily" characteristics, but elements of the human self which may be said to be a part of the "soul," such as our feelings, imagination, and reason. Body and soul, then, are not to be regarded as separate, distinct entities, but as an organic unity which stands in its totality against man's transcendent sense of perfection.

In spite of some lingering ambiguities in both traditions, the Platonic body-soul dichotomy and the related Christian flesh-spirit dichotomy may be viewed as only a symbolical rendering of a tension which is actually between man as an organic whole of body and spirit and the sense of higher destiny which is both immanent in and transcendent of the human self. "The body" and "the flesh" express symbolically the disruptive, destructive, evil inclinations of the human will as diverted from its true end.

The Logic of Participation

The task of grasping philosophically the coexistence in life of order and disorder is not made easy for the modern Westerner whose mind is steeped in the logic of modern empiricism. He will be prone to view the elements of human consciousness as "things." My explication of the paradox of dualism will seem a strange assertion of the compatibility of incompatible substances. Philosophical terms like *unity, mul-*

tiplicity, *finite*, *infinite*, and *dualism* are likely to acquire a mathematical coloring. The result will be a mental picture drastically opposed to the meaning which the various terms are intended to convey. Reifying logic will miss the point of this discussion, for the natural tendency of such logic is to reduce reality to a single level of spatial entities, whereas we are considering an irreducible spiritual paradox. The idea that the human self is at the same time and in the same respect changing and remaining the same, an ordered unity and a locus of disorder, will appear incomprehensible.

But this notion of simultaneous order and disorder is perfectly reasonable to another type of thought, the kind we use when we recognize our own enduring identity as moral subjects in the midst of a perpetually changing inner and outer life. Every new moment in a person's life is unique, and he is therefore never the same, yet he knows himself to be the same as he has always been. In grasping this fact about ourselves and others we use a type of logic which is suited to spiritual experience as we are conscious of it, not indirectly through mechanistic, quantitative analogies, but directly in our immediate awareness of reality. It is a dialectical, humanistic logic which does not try to explain away, but simply reflects, the existential tension in man between immanent and transcendent.[6]

Only if reifying thought processes are set aside for humanistic philosophy, is it possible to grasp the idea of participation (*methexis*) by which Plato gives conceptual form to the paradox of dualism. According to this idea, finite man participates in, shares in the infinite. The person who acts with a view to realizing the goal of ethical conscience be-

6 The logical problem of dualism is discussed in Leander, *Inner Check*. An important contribution toward the development of a logic appropriate to actual human experience is found in the extensive work of Benedetto Croce.

comes a part of the transcendent purpose of existence. By
striving to embody it in his personal life he brings into the
finite world a measure of harmony and order. Human activity
always remains in the realm of the imperfect, but in individuals, peoples, and civilizations inspired by the universal
good it is enlisted in a higher cause and raised to a new dignity. Through a dialectical logic, philosophy is able to give an
account of this moral synthesis.

Whereas man's ethical life is never completely ordered or
disordered, he tends to gravitate in either direction. Some
men will have but a vague conception of the moral goal for
man or lack the strength of will to adjust to its demands. To
them, more than to others, life will appear meaningless, dis-
jointed, absurd. Others will recognize ethical conscience as
pointing us towards life's fulfillment and try to live up to it.
Whereas such men will not escape all feelings of meaning-
lessness, life is likely to impress them more with its element
of enduring value. Employing the Platonic terminology, it
may be said that they are *participating* in the good.

The Higher and the Lower Self

The mysterious dualism of human life has been described by
Babbitt and More as an opposition in man between a higher
and a lower self. The latter term refers to the human will not
guided by ethical conscience. The former term, which is
synonymous with ethical conscience, refers to that in our
being which pulls us in the direction of our own true humanity, that is, towards the realization of our highest potential as
defined by a universally valid standard. Man is not merely a
set of impulses striving towards their fulfillment. There is in
him this constant stream of drives, emotions, impressions,
and ideas; as unaffected by ethical discipline and propelled by

the mood of the moment it is also called by Babbitt the "temperamental" self. But man also has a special kind of self-awareness. Not only does he have the ability to examine analytically the contents of his own consciousness, which is a rational process that need not go beyond the "lower" or "temperamental" self. He is also capable of an ethical assessment of himself. At the back of his mind the individual carries a sense of what his life should really be like. With reference to it he passes judgment on his present state and on his plans for the future. Man's ability to view life from a moral point of view is precisely what is meant by the "higher self" or, in my terminology, ethical conscience.

As a result of moral self-examination the individual may repudiate even strong inner drives in favor of what he has determined to be an *ethically* acceptable course of action. In his better moments he lets his own deepest insight into how he ought really to live prevail over the ethically unstructured inclinations of his lower self. Against the limitless possibilities for imperfection and disorder open to the individual stands the spiritual force of ethical conscience, which holds out the hope of a truly meaningful existence.

It is crucial to understand that ethical conscience is not an impulse among others. Babbitt and More express an important insight when they refer to it as "the inner check," thereby indicating that it brings order by restraining the flow of intentions. Morality is not an easy yielding to the impulse of the moment. It demands the exercise of will. Because it frequently requires the interruption or holding back of strong drives, it may involve considerable pain. The discovery of one's own moral shortcomings, which is the necessary prelude to a moral reorientation of action, is never a pleasant experience. It is not a coincidence that when the word "conscience" is used, it is most often the painful element of censure that is emphasized: "I have a bad conscience," "my conscience bothers me," "my conscience won't let me."

The point here is not that the occurrence of ethical conscience is always accompanied by pain; I shall be arguing later that allegiance to it is attended by a sense of happiness. What should be noted is that the tension within man that is introduced by ethical conscience is of a special kind. It must not be confused with the internal conflicts that grow out of the multiplicity of human drives and desires. These are frequently at cross purposes with each other, and this may indeed cause anxiety and other forms of internal strain. Tensions of that kind are not an example of moral struggle or guilt, but are contained within the lower self. The tension in man which is ethically significant is that between the infinite variety of human drives, on the one hand, and that special will in man which always wills the same moral end, on the other. In relation to the multiplicity of inclinations which make up the lower self, it is experienced as a restraining, censuring influence. [7]

Ethical conscience in one of its aspects is man's true humanity revolting against the outreaching of arbitrary impulse. Babbitt and More are severely critical of those who tend to invest the unstructured expansiveness of the human will with moral authority. "As against the expansionists of every kind," Babbitt writes, "I do not hesitate to affirm that what is

---

7 Sigmund Freud, by contrast, attempts to account for the existence of moral standards within a monistic, naturalistic framework. His notion of the superego forms part of a theory of the self-regulation of instinctual energy. Whatever the strengths or weaknesses of particular points in his psychological theories, his failure to make room for a transcendent source of morality ("We may reject the existence of an original, as it were natural, capacity to distinguish good from bad." *Civilization and Its Discontents* [New York: W. W. Norton & Co., 1962], 71) and thus recognize the essential duality of human nature is of a reductionistic variety which limits severely the value of his ideas to ethical philosophy.

specifically human in man and ultimately divine is a certain quality of will, a will that is felt in its relation to his ordinary self as a will to refrain." [8]

It should be repeated that we are now dealing with the ethical origin of order. We have opposed to it the "impulses," "spontaneity," and generally undisciplined nature of man's lower self. As has been indicated before, there is in human life not only order of an ethical kind. There may be a certain order or consistency even in the life of the most unconscionable person, who in our terminology would be ruled by his lower self. He may pursue his morally questionable goals with a high degree of efficiency and skill, giving thereby a kind of structure and coherence to his existence. In relation to the ultimate standard of human action, the ethical end, his life is disordered and undisciplined. Although in a sense his actions are not just impulsive—they are organized by the motive of efficiency—they are *ethically* unrestrained. Still, one speaks of the impulsiveness or temperamental drift of the lower self with less danger of being misunderstood when considering a life-style which, after the fashion of romantic and vitalistic philosophies, exults in spontaneous feeling and action. The fundamental distinction to be kept in mind, however, is that between a life tending towards immersion in the lower self, be it rationalistic and calculating or romantic, and an ethically disciplined life.

When using the word *impulse* I employ it in the wide sense of positive human energy, as a name for the power which carries human action, "mental" and "physical." Impulse is not understood as being necessarily blind or unthinking.

The human self, then, is a unity of two opposing wills, one of which tends to predominate. That man is repeatedly

---

8 Babbitt, *Democracy and Leadership*, 6.

drawn into disharmony and destructivity, or sin, to speak religious language, is a glaring fact of his existence. But his very awareness of evil points out the duality of his will. He could know evil will only by good will. We have not only a self which left to itself pulls us in the direction of selfish and transitory goals, but a self that wants what has intrinsic and enduring value. The higher and the lower self together form the person. Still, by the paradox of dualism only our higher will is recognized by us as the principle of our true nature. It carries a special authority, the defiance of which has special consequences, namely feelings of guilt.

One of the striking features of modern ethical thought is a tendency to declare that various human experiences are not really what they are felt to be. "Conscience," it is said, does not represent any objective principle of morality. It can be only a manifestation of subjective norms. The trouble with this and similar allegations is that they do not cover the facts. They lay claim to universal validity, but they do not explain or account for the compelling nature of the sense of moral duty experienced in conscience. If as intelligent human beings we must recognize that conscience is in actual fact "nothing but" the workings of "internalized social norms," why do we continue to behave nevertheless as if conscience had a moral authority of its own? Why do people feel guilt and self-contempt when they go against their innermost notion of how a human being ought really to live? If the modern allegations about conscience are accepted as true, those reactions can only be put down as irrational. To argue, for instance, that men respect moral norms only for fear of punishment or losing the approval of their fellow humans is simply to ignore that ethical conscience is known precisely by the fact that it compels the individual in a certain direction *regardless* of what the social expectations happen to be.

It should perhaps be repeated at this point that the nature and direction of the moral authority of conscience is not, and could not be, as readily apparent to everyone. Ethical conscience cannot be described as some sort of inner voice in each man which states mechanically and without ambiguity the moral course of action in each situation to a passively waiting individual. It is instead a sense of direction which acquires a more definite form, that is, becomes associated with a certain type of life, and reveals more of its compelling nature only as the individual makes an active effort to guide his behavior by it, a process which carries over also into his intellectual, conceptual grasp of reality. On the other hand, in the person who is more inclined towards a life of sensual gratification, emotional indulgence, or ethically uninformed rationality, it is entirely possible that the strong onrush of desire or ambition will almost drown out the "still small voice" of ethical conscience. To the extent that a person in the latter category does have moral qualms about his life, he may well be prevented by his relative lack of ethically structured experience and knowledge from identifying the root cause of his uneasiness. The nature of ethical conscience cannot be adequately grasped in isolation from the type of life which is already ordered morally and intellectually. Moral guilt can be properly recognized as such only within this ethical and conceptual frame of reference, supplied partially by traditions which incorporate a long process of culture. This is another way of saying that the nature of ethical conscience is revealed only very imperfectly and ambiguously to the person who is morally confused. In the extreme case of a person who is also mentally disordered, the problem would be compounded. The removal of confusion, then, is not a simple matter of deciding to "listen to conscience," for ethical conscience becomes known to man through a whole orientation of will and reason.

Although in its central dimension it transcends particular cultures, it remains inchoate apart from a heritage of moral and intellectual discipline. Ethical insight must be viewed as the crowning achievement of an entire cultural tradition.

Man's actual experience of ethical conscience, whether in the form of a sense of censure or approval, makes a non-subjectivistic interpretation unavoidable. By its very nature, moral guilt is a sense of having done violence to a norm that is not merely arbitrary. If the norm that has been defied were indeed only subjective, and recognizable by man as only subjective, the feeling of guilt would be a mystery. Categorical relativistic or nihilistic assertions about conscience come up against this difficulty: in the moment of guilt itself at least, men are not able to convince themselves of the truth of that view of morals. The guilt is *there*. The feeling *is* a sense of having violated a sacred purpose. No amount of abstract explanation which may later be tacked on to the experience can change the sense itself. The allegation that conscience is in reality nothing more than a mere code word for subjectivism of one kind or another leaves its moral *authority* unexplained.

Moral self-contempt and reassurance show up the duality of the self and the existence of a true human identity. We are not just playing with words when we think and speak of ourselves in a dualistic manner: "I am not myself," "I betrayed my own conscience," "I pulled myself together." By a certain abstract, formal type of logic this use of the word "I" is blatantly contradictory, but by the logic of actual human self-awareness it presents no problem. We *are* beings of two selves. In More's formulation: "We do not know the flux by the inner check, or the inner check by the flux, or either of these by some other element of our being, but we are immediately and inexplicably conscious of both at once—we are both at once." [9] At the same time, only the inner check can be said to be man's true self. [10]

Ethical Conscience as Censure and Purpose

Morality points man beyond the flux of changing circumstances. Although finite, man is aware in ethical conscience of a transcendent destiny. Adjusting his life to this lasting goal, he reproduces in this world a measure of that order which he knows as the essence of life. We need to look closer at the process whereby moral order is brought into the finite world. How does the individual come to participate in the good?

Let it be suggested that moral choice begins in a doubt. The idea of an alternative line of action does not occur to a person as long as he has no question about the rightness of his present conduct. All of a sudden, however, there may come to him the feeling that what he is doing or about to do is fraught with moral danger. Where before there was unquestioning activity, there is moral uncertainty. He is confronted by an inhibition, an uneasy sense that performance of the intended act would violate a sacred principle. A tension has appeared between what he is planning to do and what he ought to do. It has struck a pause in the flow of impulses embodying his original plan. Instead of steady, uninterrupted activity

9 Paul Elmer More, "Definitions of Dualism," in *The Drift of Romanticism*, Vol. VIII of *Shelburne Essays* (11 vols.; New York: Phaeton Press, 1967), 249.
10 *Cf.* Romans, 7:19–23. "For the good that I would I do not: but the evil which I would not, that I do. Now if I do that I would not, it is no more I that do it, but sin that dwelleth in me. I find then a law that, when I would do good, evil is present with me. For I delight in the law of God after the inward man: But I see another law in my members, warring against the law of my mind, and bringing me into captivity to the law of sin which is in my members."

there is a doubt. The halting of outgoing impulses allows the person an opportunity to scrutinize and reevaluate his intentions. A new perspective has been opened up in the light of which he may contemplate alternative lines of action. The essential fact about the inner monologue which is triggered by moral doubt is that it is guided by this motive: a *moral* course must be sought. The inhibition which sets him deliberating consists in the recognition that this motive was lacking in or unsuccessfully applied to his original plan.

A person who acts on the opportunity afforded him by moral doubt will, if he is lucky, come up with a course of action which is not censured, as was his old one, by nagging dissatisfaction. He will feel morally reassured. New determination will fill him. Action is released. The set of impulses which embody the new plan are felt by him to be in consonance with his true purpose as a human being. He is not acting arbitrarily, but with a view to the universal good for man.

A present act or plan of action is thus censured by a pang of moral doubt. This interference with outgoing impulse is what Babbitt and More call "the inner check." It establishes a contrast between ethically unordered activity and the higher goal intended for man. There is, let it be repeated, considerable significance in saying that this end is apparent to man in the form of a "check," "inhibition," or "negation." These terms indicate that ethical conscience is not just one human drive among others which sometimes manages to overpower competing impulses. It is not possible to explain ethical order as the self-regulation of impulse. Such an attempt ultimately ends up in clearly unsatisfactory notions of instinctual guidance, which ignore the human reality of conscious intent. Ethical conscience is an interference "from without" with positive human energy. It can order action, because it transcends it. Belonging to the realm of the infinite, it is experienced by man with reference to the end-less variety of finite ideas and desires as a principle of moderation or censure; it wills not the multiplicity of imperfect human acts but the perfection of the ethical end by means of an ordering of multiplicity.

Nothing could be more tempting than to believe that one's own inclinations carry the authority of divine command. Moral theories which tend to regard man's spontaneous wishes as the voice of God have the double attraction of flattering the individual and relieving him of the need to exert the will. Not only is ethical conscience not to be identified with impulse, it is doubtful that it can be identified with positive human intentions at all. Human actions and plans are finite, ethical conscience an expression of infinite will. For that reason it cannot really be said, except in a special sense, that ethical conscience gives specific commands. The person who thinks that he is positively ordered to perform this or that act needs to remember that while his *motive* may be that of ethical conscience, concrete human acts fall short of perfection. Man's higher self points him in a definite direction, that of the moral end, but it does not assure attainment of the goal.

Ethical conscience makes us aware that we must not act arbitrarily, pursuing our own selfish interests or those of our own group, but that we must instead act morally, seeking the common good which transcends particularistic wishes. It wants our every action to advance that purpose. The ethical course of action, however, is not revealed to us in the form of concrete, detailed prescriptions for the given circumstances. To discern what is moral in the particular situation may require considerable deliberation. Even the person who is truly inspired by the motive to act morally may fail in his purpose, for the successful planning and execution of action involves not only a motivating principle, but pragmatic reason together with a factual grasp of the pertinent circumstances. As Aristotle points out, "goodness in itself is not enough; there must also be the power to translate it into action." [11] However powerful a man's reason or plentiful his knowledge, he can never predict with certainty the consequences of his actions. To be able to achieve at least some success in finding the moral course a person must not only have the right motive, but wisdom and prudence regarding ends and means.

Strictly speaking, then, ethical conscience only reveals the *spirit* in which we must apply our mental and physical resources. Moral behavior is a human creation conceived under its guidance. That does not mean that the standard of morality is subjective. Ethical conscience always wills a definite course of action, the one most conducive to good, and motivates man to seek it, only the individual has to discover its concrete form in the particular case.

Ethical conscience is not only a principle of censure. If it were, it would be a mere negation of human life, demanding asceticism or even death. As already indicated, it is also felt by man as a sense of spiritual purpose. It does not always manifest itself as a check on impulse. It gives a kind of approval to certain actions by withholding its censure. Having first bothered an individual with moral doubt, a sense of threat to his higher destiny as man, it may then suddenly lift its ban when a new course of action is contemplated. That is another way of saying that it gives a kind of sanction to it. The intended action and its foreseen consequences are felt to *participate* in man's moral purpose. A set of impulses are, as it were, endowed with the tacit endorsement of the higher self. In this special sense, and then only if it is remembered that

11 Aristotle, *The Politics*, trans. T. A. Sinclair (Harmondsworth: Penguin Books, 1962), 263.

the action may not in the end produce the intended result, it may be permissible to say that ethical conscience "commands" certain actions. The idea of a moral command needs to be understood in conjunction with the idea that ethical conscience is also that in man which predisposes against premature certainty regarding the morality of specific acts.[12]

The Paradox of Moral Freedom

We are approaching the very center of the paradox of dualism: moral freedom. Man must act to realize his sacred destiny, but the freedom to do so both is and is not of his own making.

Going about his business a person is suddenly aware that he is free to repudiate his present intentions. There is a recognition that he is now moving towards a morally questionable goal. Where there was smug complacency or a blind pursuit of ethically unworthy ends, there is an opportunity to reevaluate and reconstruct. In one sense, the freedom to recover one's moral purpose is not of man's own making. It is there, a free gift to accept or reject. It seems appropriate in this context to speak of grace. It should be noted that this opportunity to choose is indissolubly bound up with a sense of higher purpose. The moment of moral choice is not an open-ended predicament. Whenever we say moral freedom, we also say moral duty or responsibility, for its origin is the interruption of impulse by ethical conscience. Man can perhaps be said to be "on his own" in that he does not any longer have

12 My notion of ethical conscience, then, should not be confused with a type of moral "intuitionism" which ascribes to specific moral judgments a self-evident, incontrovertible character. What can be said to be "self-evident" according to my theory is not ordinarily the morality of this or that act but the *obligation* to seek the moral course. *Cf.* Mary Warnock, *Ethics Since 1900* (London: Oxford University Press, 1960), 56–78.

to follow his previous plan. But the stirring of ethical conscience is by its very nature a call to respond affirmatively. The
individual is invited to act morally. His freedom consists in
being able to take advantage of the opportunity. To resign it is
merely to revert to the tyranny of spiritually destructive actions and their necessary consequences. That means giving
up moral freedom. In the most profound sense of the term,
that freedom is to act in accordance with the true end for
man. The term does not signify that man is somehow left to
carve out his own destiny in a morally undetermined universe. The end of ethical conscience is sacred and compelling. Its authority can be defied, but not repealed.

The paradox of moral freedom has another aspect. The
moral person does not passively wait for ethical conscience to
interfere with those of his impulses which embody an unethical plan. Although transcendent of finite human reality,
ethical conscience should not only be viewed as ordering life
from the "outside." It is the higher self of acting human persons. The moral man is striving to be moral. Although he
knows that he may be censured when he least expects it, he
proceeds on the premise that by trying to act morally he will
actually come closer to the goal. In Christian language, one
might say that he believes that those who seek shall find.

The moral man does not act at random. From ethical experience he knows that man's true humanity lies in one direction rather than another. He has a memory of being censured or reassured when acting in certain ways. As a result of
innumerable choices in the past, his personality has been
aimed in such a direction as to avoid some of the more obvious
pitfalls. Also, he is not solely dependent on private experience. He has access to the general experience of mankind as
reflected in long-honored ethical norms. These sources of
moral insight form the basis for the development of habits
which build a certain ethical momentum into his character.

But what does it mean to *try* to act morally? It means not to go ahead before having asked the question, "Is this plan moral?" It means to put oneself in the frame of mind in which the voice of ethical conscience will not be drowned out by the onrush of strong desire. But the very opportunity to scrutinize intentions from this higher point of view before letting them pass into action presupposes a reprieve from the flow of ethically unstructured impulse. It requires the occurrence of the inner check. When we talk of *trying* to act morally, therefore, we are actually already talking about man acting from inside his higher self. By the paradox of dualism, a person's sincere wish to act morally is already an opportunity to do so. The wish itself is a manifestation of ethical conscience. In a sense, moral inspiration cannot be commanded. It is there, or it is not. But, by the paradox of dualism, it will come to him who seeks it.

Morality as Happiness

The preceding argument has been an attempt to describe man's moral predicament. It has focused on how ethical conscience orders human life. Since the discussion has been largely formal, nagging questions of this kind will be lurking in the background: "But what, in substantive terms, is the good?" "What, specifically, is a moral and immoral principle of conduct?" These questions raise an inexhaustible subject. To even begin to answer them it would be necessary to relate our notion of ethical conscience to the moral traditions of mankind. The Westerner is particularly indebted for his knowledge of what is moral to the classical and Judaeo-Christian body of experience and speculation. The Oriental has available to him sources of insight of similar depth and penetration. What we are exploring here, however, is not so much the normative content of particular acts of ethical con-

science as its way of operation. Morality may be described as
a progressive discovery of good in changing circumstances. It
is dependent on a dynamic interplay of ethical conscience, as
experienced directly by the individual in particular situations, and the moral insights of humanity, as reflected in
long-respected ethical norms. I have been trying to describe
the *process* whereby ethical conscience reveals man's transcendent destiny.

But the workings of ethical conscience are indistinguishable from the intrinsic value of its operation. I have hinted
throughout at the positive content of its effects in the use of
such words as *meaning, harmony*, and *worth*. I shall try to
show later that ethical conscience is the origin of genuine social community. Even with much longer explications of these
terms than can be given here, it would not be possible to
show what the good is in itself. The good is that in terms of
which everything else is defined. Although manifested in particular acts, it transcends all individual circumstances. The
issue of what the good is substantively can be dealt with up to
a point by philosophical argument, but has to be settled
finally in practice, in concrete moral experience. I recognize
that without eliciting the proper referents in experience what
little has been said and will be said on the subject here is
likely to seem thin and abstract.

The primary objective is to describe the *form* taken by ethical activity, but some additional remarks regarding the positive content of such activity may help shed more light on the
nature of ethical conscience. Man's higher will is in one of its
aspects a sense of spiritual direction. In the person who is
continually trying to order his life by it, it may be described as
a sense of happiness. The latter word has been cheapened by
association with romantic sentimentalism and utilitarianism
and by the general vulgarization of terms. It is used here
roughly in the sense given it by Aristotle.

There are innumerable standards by which one may assess the quality of life, such as economic well-being, personal freedom, security, and sensual satisfaction. All of these can be regarded as measures of good. The central concern of ethical philosophy is the ultimate principle with reference to which the relative goodness of everything else may be judged. Aristotle observes that all human activity aims at some good. All goods, however, are not of the same rank. Among ends available to man that is superior to all others which is sought for its own sake. "We call final without qualification that which is always desirable in itself and never for the sake of something else." Aristotle clarifies by adding: "Honour, pleasure, reason, and every virtue we choose indeed for themselves (for if nothing resulted from them we should still choose each of them), but we choose them also for the sake of happiness, judging that by means of them we shall be happy. Happiness, on the other hand, no one chooses for the sake of these, nor, in general, for anything other than itself." [13]

Set above competing goods there is thus a standard, definable in one of its aspects as happiness, in terms of which everything else must be evaluated. Something is good, in the strict sense of the word, to the extent that it contributes to happiness. It is essential to point out that happiness as Aristotle understands it is not simply a feeling of well-being among others. It is a special kind of awareness beyond particular acts and their respective satisfactions. The successful completion of action always results in some sort of pleasure, just as the interruption of action always causes some pain. That is true also of moral acts. There is a sense of pleasure that attends their completion which is not happiness, but only a passing feeling of satisfaction. Happiness is the awareness of the unvarying element in morality, of the good itself,

13 Aristotle, *The Nicomachean Ethics*, trans. David Ross (London: Oxford University Press, 1954), 11 (1097a), 12 (1097b).

in which individual moral acts are only participating. It is the sense of meaning and worth which is intrinsic to a whole life orientation, marked by continuous effort to seek not transitory, particularistic, selfish ends, but the enduring, universal, ethical end known in ethical conscience. The happy man is not an Epicurean skillfully maximizing pleasure and minimizing pain. Neither is he an ascetic who renounces all pleasure. He is the man who finds pleasure in the right things: "Those things are both valuable and pleasant which are such to the good man." [14]

In accordance with this important distinction between happiness and pleasure, it is quite possible for a moral person to be deprived of success in his dealings and thus also of pleasure, and still be happy, because of the intrinsic value of the orientation of his character. Plato describes the lot of the true philosophers who in a decadent age are denied the influence which is their due: "They'll find no ally to save them in the fight for justice; and if they're not prepared to join others in their wickedness, and yet are unable to fight the general savagery single-handed, they are likely to perish like a man thrown among wild beasts, without profit to themselves or others, before they can do any good to their friends or society." In spite of the fact that the good life is thwarted around them, happiness is not beyond their reach, for their own commitment to the good is not diminished by their lack of success in influencing their contemporaries. Having sought to keep themselves "unspotted from wickedness and wrong in this life," they will "finally leave it with cheerful composure and good hope." [15] The most striking illustration of the same idea would be the martyred saint. Conversely, a person may

14 *Ibid.*, 262 (1176b).
15 Plato, *The Republic*, trans. H. D. P. Lee (Rev. ed; Harmondsworth: Penguin Books, 1974), 292.

be highly successful in realizing his plans and thus live a life of pleasure, and yet be unhappy, because of the low moral quality of his goals. It should be added that according to Plato and Aristotle pleasure and happiness tend to go together in the good man under normal circumstances.

To counter a possible misunderstanding, it needs to be made clear that Aristotle does not regard happiness as some sort of passive state. "We must," he says, "class happiness as an activity." [16] His view of the proper end for man can be summed up by saying that it consists in a special type of activity which makes man happy. "To each man there comes just so much happiness as he has of moral and intellectual goodness and of performance of actions dependent thereon." [17] Such activity, in other words, is its own reward. It is "something final and self-sufficient, and is the end of action." [18] Because Aristotle calls the very culmination of this activity "the contemplative life," the modern student accustomed to a nonclassical conception of reason stands in danger of underestimating its ethical element. The activity of the good man is first and foremost a process of moral betterment.

The ascent to happiness is a difficult and protracted one. It requires a steady commitment to virtuous action. "For one swallow does not make a summer, nor does one day; and so too one day, or a short time, does not make a man blessed and happy." Aristotle distinguishes between three levels of human life. The lowest, which is preferred by "men of the most vulgar type," does not aim beyond the pursuit of pleasure. [19] Superior to it is what he calls the "political" life, which presupposes considerable moral attainment among the

16 Aristotle, *Nicomachean Ethics*, 261 (1176b).
17 Aristotle, *Politics*, 257.
18 Aristotle, *Nicomachean Ethics*, 12 (1097b).
19 *Ibid.*, 14 (1098a), 6 (1095b).

citizens of the state and enlists prosperity and other goods as means in the cause of the good life. Higher still, too high, indeed, for all but a very few, is the contemplative life, that in which happiness is achieved to the fullest, as far as it is humanly possible. It requires only a minimum of worldly goods. This highest level of life has many important points of contact with the Christian notion of saintliness.

It should be emphasized that happiness is conceived by Aristotle as a social, communal value. It is self-sufficient, not in the sense that it is "sufficient for a man by himself, for one who lives a solitary life, but also for parents, children, wife, and in general for his friends and fellow citizens, since man is born for citizenship." [20] Aristotle's idea of happiness cannot be distinguished from his idea of true friendship, which may be defined as partnership in the good life, a state possible only between men of virtue.

The Aristotelian notion of a self-justifying higher activity, which is a realization of life's true end and accompanied by happiness, is closely analogous to the Christian notion of love. It is the good for the sake of which all other goods are, or ought to be, sought. It is manifested in man's life in its highest dimension "in so far as something divine is present in him." [21] At this point the religious person will want to put his own theological interpretation on the terms. Because it is not necessary for my present purpose, I shall refrain, however, from taking up a theological line of argument.

20 *Ibid.*, 12, (1097b).
21 *Ibid.*, 265 (1177b).

The Ethics of Community

Man is by nature a social being, said the classical Greek philosophers. They are joined in that view by Christian thinkers. It has been a fundamental tenet of the tradition resulting from these sources that social life aims beyond cooperation for the attainment of material well-being and social peace to the realization of the good life. Against the background of the above analysis we are better able to understand the process by which this goal is approached.

I have argued that man is capable of cooperation because of his ability to think symbolically. This ability , which makes possible the planning and organization of activity, is a necessary prerequisite for all social life. Indeed, I have indicated that symbolical thought, which is the distinctively human mode of consciousness, is in essence a social faculty; symbols are not private possessions but detached meanings usable in isolation from the experience to which they refer. It has also been observed that social cooperation has as one of its origins a purely selfish wish to escape the grimmer aspects of the war of all against all. To that argument I have added the important point that without the recognition of an ethical, that is, self-justifying, goal above competing interests, social peace will be highly precarious and ultimately succumb to the centrifugal forces of partisan wills. It remains to be discussed how man realizes the good life. It is primarily of man's capacity to achieve that goal that the classical and Christian political philosophers are thinking when they assert that man is by nature social. Because they are concerned not simply with social living, but with the good life, questions of ethics take precedence.

Social life may be viewed as promoting a wide array of activities and corresponding values. These can be classed as ethical, intellectual, aesthetic, and economic,[1] with politics defined as cutting across these lines. By a civilized society I mean one where these pursuits have attained a high level. Since the worth of everything must ultimately be judged by its contribution to the final purpose of life, civilization first and foremost signifies ethical attainment. The intellectual, aesthetic, and economic life of a society may be said to be truly civilized to the degree that these activities serve the ethical goal. While their respective values of truth, beauty, and economy (efficiency) have their own organizing principle or intrinsic standard of perfection, they fulfill their highest role only as they advance the purpose of the ethical. By this definition, a society which has reached a high level of efficiency in attaining its goals, but whose efficiency does not measurably serve the realization of moral ends, would not be civilized in the full sense of the word. The point is vividly illustrated by the early success of the Nazi war machine. Simi-

---

1 This way of categorizing human activity is suggested by Benedetto Croce. See his *The Philosophy of the Practical*, trans. Douglas Ainslie (New York: Biblo and Tannen, 1967). The reader should be cautioned against the weaknesses of this translation.

   In adopting Croce's four categories, I am not also accepting his monistic philosophical premises. The question may also be asked if his categories give a truly exhaustive account of human life. If they cover the level of life which Aristotle calls "political" and Irving Babbitt calls "humanistic" or "civilized," do they also cover completely what is above that level of life, namely, saintliness?

larly, a society which exhibits a high degree of intellectual activity but devotes little of it to discovering the conditions of the ethical life would be only marginally civilized. The moral goal for society to which all other goals are subservient and of which they are ideally supportive we may call community.

I have argued that man is torn between spiritually disruptive and unifying inclinations. In a social context, the disintegrative pull of a person's lower self will put him in conflict with his fellow men. His own particularistic wishes will clash with those of others. An uneasy social peace may be maintained through the restraint suggested by enlightened self-interest, but to the extent that men lead ethically undisciplined lives, community in the real sense of the word will be impossible. Community can emerge only in a society where the forces of egotistical interests are tempered by concern for the common good.

By disposing us against what is merely arbitrary and selfish, ethical conscience disposes against what separates us from others. It wills, not what is in the private interest of certain individuals or groups, but what is good for its own sake. That end is at the same time the good for the individual and the good for all. To the extent, therefore, that men are ruled by ethical conscience, they are unified with others. Just as, in the individual, moral discipline produces a self-justifying integration of the personality, in society it produces a self-justifying harmony. Community is human association under the guidance of ethical conscience. Man's true humanity is realized by being shared. It should be understood that community is experienced between those who order their lives with reference to the same universal moral authority. A moral person who refuses to participate in immorality around him may well become isolated or separated. The opposite of separation in this case, however, would not be community.

In one sense, man's effort to achieve the good life can be said to be an individualistic undertaking. It is centered in a moral authority of which the individual is directly aware in himself. It is felt to be so closely associated with his own essential identity that it may be called his higher self. He realizes his true purpose by heeding the Socratic-Delphic admonition to "know thyself." Also, moral betterment can come about only through personal acts of will. But the type of individualism I am describing has nothing to do with an atomistic view of man and society. The process of spiritual development always points beyond individual personality. Man's higher self is not some private reality but the potential for true humanity shared by all. Its authority is universal, that is, nonindividualistic. It is binding on and has effects on all men. This argument is closely related to Aristotle's teaching about true friendship. In Aristotle's view the latter presupposes some considerable moral elevation among the participants. Because ethical conscience wills the same ultimate end in all men, it can be said with Aristotle that the moral individual "is related to his friend as to himself." [2]

The individual person is unique, not by virtue of his higher self, but by the meeting in his being of the infinite as known in ethical conscience and the finite as manifested in his particular personal characteristics. Since men live under different circumstances and have different capabilities, ethical conscience does not call men to identical lives. The professor will be able to advance the cause of man's true humanity in other ways than the priest or the businessman, to take just three examples having to do with the individual's occupation. What should be carefully noted is that the higher self enlists

2 Aristotle, *The Nichomachean Ethics*, trans. David Ross (London: Oxford University Press, 1954), 228 (1166a). Aristotle's theory of friendship is developed primarily in Books VIII an IX.

the uniqueness of each person in one and the same moral cause, as far, that is, as that uniqueness is compatible with the cause. Whatever the particular circumstances, the goal is always this: extending the influence of the ethical will.

Community, then, is experienced, not between skillfully calculating egotists, or, for that matter, between mere "lovers of humanity" lacking in understanding of man's spiritual nature and destiny, but between individuals who are trying to rise above whatever is separative and disruptive in their characters to what is highest in each of them. The life they attain is not based on subjective whim, but on the supra-individual authority of ethical conscience. They are ordering their lives with reference to a "centre of judgment set above the shifting impressions of the individual and the flux of phenomenal nature."[3] They are unified with each other through loyalty to a self which is the same in all men. In religious terminology, they are unified in the will of God.

In the context of community, the common good is not merely a code word for successful compromise between clashing selfish interests. It refers to the element in human interaction which transcends private advantage. Such is the nature of a living together at a level of some ethical nobility supported by general cultural elevation. This type of life, although personally satisfying to the individuals comprising it, does not need to be defended by arguments of self-interest. It is its own justification. Whatever contributes to it can be supported, not because it happens to serve the interests of this or that individual or group, but because it fulfills an intrinsically valuable existence. It is the societal end for which the civilized man knows that he is intended. In community, men have been brought together at a common center of val-

3 Irving Babbitt, *Democracy and Leadership* (New York: Houghton Mifflin Co., 1924), 9.

ues. In Aristotelian terminology that center is happiness or true friendship, in Christian terminology, love.

It should be added that while community is the ethical goal of society, it is not to be understood as one which could be completely attained. That would presuppose the disappearance of selfish motives from the face of the earth. To the extent that it is realized, community will have to coexist with egotism. Drawing on our previous discussion of the relationship between morality and self-interest,[4] we can say that the pursuit of private advantage can never become morality. To a certain extent, however, it can be bent to fit the purposes of the moral life by the ethical forces of community in the surrounding society, which subject selfishness to a degree of control. To take an example, a businessman concerned only with his own well-being and pleasure and trying to make a profit to further that end may under certain cultural circumstances still help to advance a higher goal. Provided that the market demand to which he is responding is itself cultured and at least partially due to a wish on the part of the buyers to realize moral ends, the businessman's desire to make a profit, which is the reward for having served the consumer efficiently, may actually give some support to the ethical life of society. In spite of the low moral quality of his own ultimate motive, higher goals are served by his economic risk taking and imagination. Or consider a power-hungry democratic politician who has no other motive for his participation in politics than to enhance his personal influence. In spite of himself, he may in his opportunistic pandering to the voters actually serve morality, provided that the wishes of his supporters have some ethical merit.[5]

4 See Chapter I herein, pp. 20–26.
5 Needless to say, the implication here is not that businessmen are necessarily embodiments of greed or politicians the personification of an all-consuming lust for power.

The Ethical Life and Tradition

In the course of man's search for his own true humanity there slowly emerges a general sense as to what types of activity contribute to the goal and detract from it. In a society which takes that search seriously, mankind's historical experience will be a valued source of insight and guidance to be drawn upon in the development of specific norms of upbringing and education, of intellectual, artistic, and political activity. All of these will help to buttress the kind of humane social interaction which is ultimately dependent on individual efforts of will. In such a society tradition becomes both an expression of and support for the good life. It helps direct man's will and imagination towards his enduring spiritual purpose. It is a molding, formative force checking the spontaneous growth of premature, misguided opinion and behavior. One might say that in encouraging in the individual a certain steadiness of action tradition serves to make the good life habitual. And according to Aristotle, "Moral virtue comes about as a result of habit." [6]

It should be carefully noted that, although invaluable as a guide to the good life, tradition never gives final expression to man's higher destiny. Sound tradition grows out of an effort to give positive content to man's sense of spiritual purpose, but that sense ultimately transcends all specific human forms. Yet, the good life is unthinkable outside of tradition. Imperfect man is capable of attaining civilization only because he is born into a cultural context which incorporates the experience and insight of his predecessors. The good life is a communal creation, not only in the sense that it entails cooperation of the living, but because it involves the efforts of previous generations. Still, because of the imperfection of all

6 Aristotle, *Nicomachean Ethics*, 28 (1103a).

human accomplishments and changing circumstances, genuinely beneficial traditionalism is not an unbending insistence on the status quo. Attempts to put the spirit of civilization in a cultural straitjacket will stifle and perhaps even kill it. Conventional beliefs and norms must be continually evaluated with reference to man's direct knowledge of the purpose that they are supposed to advance.

It is entirely consistent that those who come to value cultural tradition the most are frequently the same who stress the need for an imaginative and critical assessment of contemporary society. Among them is Edmund Burke. His combination of a respect for ancient custom and willingness to challenge the ways of present society is apparent in his classical statement of the primary qualification of a statesman, "a disposition to preserve, and an ability to improve." The same outlook is reflected in Burke's statement that "a state without the means of some change is without the means of its conservation." [7] Similar views are expressed by one of Burke's leading American disciples, Russell Kirk. He writes: "In a healthy nation, tradition must be balanced by some strong element of curiosity and individual dissent." [8] It must not be ignored that "the world does change; a certain sloughing off of tradition and prescription is at work in any vigorous society, and a certain adding to the bulk of received opinion goes on from age to age." [9]

Strong challenges are sometimes mounted in particular societies against the cultural traditions that have long sustained

7 Edmund Burke, *Reflections on the Revolution in France* (London: Everyman's Library, 1964), 153, 19.
8 Russell Kirk, *A Program for Conservatives* (Chicago: Henry Regnery Co., 1954), 305.
9 Russell Kirk, "Prescription, Authority and Ordered Freedom," in Frank S. Meyer (ed.), *What Is Conservatism?* (New York: Holt, Rinehart & Winston, 1964), 31.

them. The problem then becomes to determine whether the attempted break with long-respected principles is indeed the result of new, superior insight or merely the result of a failure to absorb the cultural heritage, a slackening of the will and the ability to live up to the high demands of true civilization. This task of evaluation, it is evident, requires not only familiarity with the new beliefs, but a thorough understanding of the ancient traditions which have allegedly been supplanted.

What is to be preserved, then, is not tradition as an imperfect human creation, but a living awareness of man's higher destiny. The sign of a creative culture would be that it manages to weed out that in its traditions which is only temporally conditioned, transitory, or of marginal value and keep strong that which speaks to man's central and enduring concerns. The principles of the good life tend to become reflected in tradition, for they represent the permanent element in history amid the flux of continual change. Sound tradition, as opposed to mere cultural inertia, is the ethical, intellectual, artistic, and political expression of what man has found to fulfill his own humanity. The civilized human being is the beneficiary of the historical process to substitute for what is only transitory in human attachments that which has enduring meaning and worth. To relate this point to the Platonic notion of the one and the many, which has supplied the theme for our discussion of the ethical life, tradition is a part of man's attempt to maintain his grasp of the oneness in the infinite variety of human experience.

PART THREE

Rousseau's General Will: Moral Fact or Utopian Fiction?

The Political Moralism
of Rousseau

V

Having developed with some care the idea of the duality of
human nature and the relation of ethical conscience to community and culture, we are in a position to examine in depth
the implications of man's moral predicament for the theory of
democracy. The ethical reasoning should now be applied to
the difficult question of which institutional arrangements
can make popular rule compatible with the promotion of the
ethical life. Our moral framework established, we shall turn
to a consideration of one of the most influential answers to
that question in Western political thought, that given by
Jean-Jacques Rousseau in *The Social Contract*. An analysis of
Rousseau's argument is suggested by the fact that he is
widely regarded as a founder of modern democratic thought
and by the fact that, directly or indirectly, his ideas form an
important part of the hidden assumptions of much political
theory in the twentieth century. My examination of the doctrine of majority rule propounded by this seminal thinker is
intended to bring some of those assumptions into the open
and to expose certain central ethical problems which are usually blurred or evaded in modern thought.

The following analysis of Rousseau's theory of popular rule
will help to develop a fundamental distinction which, although crucial to democratic theory, is only vaguely recog-

nized and understood by most influential theoreticians of democracy today. In his effort to reconcile ethics and politics Rousseau becomes the champion of a form of popular rule which may be termed "plebiscitary democracy," one which gives maximum freedom and power to the momentary majority of the people by placing no strongly resistant legal obstacles in the way of emerging popular wishes. This type of democracy may be defined in contradistinction to "constitutional democracy," a form of popular rule designed to promote, not the instant and complete public implementation of the most recent will of the people, but the articulation of the "deliberate sense" of the community, to use a phrase from the American constitutional tradition. Popular majorities are subject to constitutional restraints whose removal requires an elaborate procedure and not only persistent but overwhelming popular support. The purpose of such a form of government is to filter out what is merely transitory or premature in the various expressions of popular will and to enhance the implementation of what is lasting and well considered. These, it may be argued, are two essentially different conceptions of democracy with vastly different ethical implications. They delineate what may well be the fundamental theoretical alternative available to proponents of popular rule. Intelligent choice between them requires a choice between conflicting ethical philosophies. To be able to evaluate the validity of Rousseau's germinal theory of plebiscitary democracy we must carefully examine its ethical foundations.

A thorough analysis of Rousseau's ideas about popular rule is more than appropriate, since his thinking involves a few important concepts and terms which bear a certain resemblance to some of those advanced in this discussion. I have introduced the idea of a higher and a lower self in man, hinting at the possibility of applying it to a whole people. It has been indicated that the higher self, or ethical conscience, is not a merely private, subjective will, but a will common to all men. Rousseau, by way of comparison, distinguishes in *The Social Contract* and elsewhere between the general will (*la volonté générale*), which he defines as the intrinsically moral will of the people, and the will of all (*la volonté de tous*), which is a mere aggregation of their selfish interests. He also speaks of a people's common self (*moi commun*). It needs to be determined whether these similarities are substantive or just terminological and superficial.

Rousseau's argument for plebiscitary popular rule in *The Social Contract* turns on the notion of the general will. The task will be to decide if this concept gives an accurate account of the possible meeting of politics and morality in a democracy. Is the general will the absolute principle of right that would justify the total freedom and loyalty that Rousseau claims for it? On the answer to this question depends the adequacy of the institutional arrangements for popular rule which he suggests.

I hope to show that there are grave objections to accepting Rousseau's general will as a guiding principle of democratic theory. It is not to be mistaken for the higher will in man, which I have called ethical conscience and to which popular rule should properly be adjusted. The thrust of Rousseau's writings is the rejection of the type of dualistic philosophy I have outlined and the affirmation of the essential unity and goodness of human nature. Morality in his thought is synonymous with uninhibited impulse. His idea of the general will and his endorsement of majority rule without constitutional restraints, I shall be arguing, rest on an illegitimate identification of morality with the immanent reality of spontaneously emerging popular wishes.

If Rousseau's thought can be said to involve any notion of

philosophical dualism, it is of a very different kind from the one I have described. For the existential, ineradicable tension in man between a transcendent ethical purpose and contrary inclinations, he substitutes a tension between man and the institutions of conventional society, which places the source of evil somehow outside of the essence of human nature. Writes Robert Nisbet: "Rousseau is the first of the modern philosophers to see in the State a means of resolving the conflicts, not merely among institutions, but within the individual himself." [1] Rousseau's rejection of constitutional limitations on the will of the people is indissolubly bound up with a failure to face the moral conflict inside the human soul.

The force of tradition is strong, however, and it causes in Rousseau's writings a measure of ambiguity. Irving Babbitt, one of his severest critics, freely admits: "That there is some survival of the older dualism in Rousseau is beyond question." [2] Spread out in his works are sentences which point beyond and even contradict the normal tendency of his philosophy. Although recognizing this strain, I shall be arguing that in the main the concept of the general will exemplifies the movement away from a transcendent standard of ethics and towards the identification of morality with politics. Rousseau himself admits to basing *The Social Contract* on the belief that "everything is rooted in politics and that, whatever might be attempted, no people would ever be other than the nature of their government made them." [3] His emphasis on the importance of politics might seem to put him close to

1 Robert Nisbet, *Community and Power* (New York: Oxford University Press, 1962), 140.
2 Irving Babbitt, *Democracy and Leadership* (New York: Houghton Mifflin Co., 1924), 76.
3 Jean-Jacques Rousseau, *The Confessions*, trans. J. M. Cohen (Harmondsworth: Penguin Books, 1953), Bk. IX, 377.

Plato and Aristotle, but there are crucial differences stem-
ming from very different views of human nature.

The concept of the general will is developed with the most
thoroughness in *The Social Contract*. Brief though it is, this
treatise contains a wealth of ideas, and also ambiguities and
contradictions, which here can only be dealt with in part and
to the exclusion of important points. It may be argued, on the
other hand, that an analysis focused on the general will takes
one to the very heart of Rousseau's political thought. While
The Social Contract will be our primary point of reference, it
is not possible to understand fully its line of argument without also consulting some of his other works. The general will
needs to be put in the proper philosophical context. This requires a somewhat roundabout approach to the basic text, including some extensive introductory remarks.

Rousseau insisted to the end on the basic philosophical
unity of his writings. He is supported in this regard by
numerous commentators who at the same time point to in-
consistencies and tensions inside this larger unity. The underlying theme of his works is described by Rousseau himself
in *Rousseau Judges Jean-Jacques*, where his interlocutor, sur-
veying Rousseau's books, sees "everywhere the development
of this great principle that nature made men happy and good,
but that society depraves him and makes him miserable." [4] In
The Social Contract, which is actually devoted to the proposition that there is one type of society that does not have this effect on man, the same theme is developed with a twist.

The basic unity of Rousseau's works is indicated in other
ways. In one passage among many where he asserts the close
ties between our central text and other books, he writes that
"all that is challenging in *The Social Contract* had previously

---

4 Jean-Jacques Rousseau, *Oeuvres Complètes* (4 vols.; Paris: Bibliothèque de la
   Pléiade, 1959–64), I, 934. Translated in Roger D. Masters, *The Political
   Philosophy of Rousseau* (Princeton: Princeton University Press, 1968), xiii.

appeared in the *Essay on Inequality*."[5] In *Emile* one finds a summary of the arguments that were later to be published in *The Social Contract*. Of the latter Rousseau writes that it "should be considered as a kind of appendix" to *Emile* and that the two works "together make a single whole."[6] It becomes still more difficult to regard *The Social Contract* as breaking in central respects with the rest of his thinking when one considers that under the preliminary title of *Political Institutions* he worked on it for over ten years, during which time he wrote other major works. Far from regarding it as some sort of deviation from his normal philosophical path, he thought of it as the treatise that would "put the seal" on his reputation.[7]

Rousseau the Man and the Thinker

It is possible to shed light on Rousseau's arguments in *The Social Contract* by drawing on his autobiographical writings as well as his formal treatises. It has been often commented upon that it is difficult, or even impossible, in the case of Rousseau to distinguish between these two types of writing. His frank descriptions of his "private" life and thoughts must be regarded, in part at least, as statements of his philosophy of life. According to Judith Shklar, for instance, the *Confessions* are of "utmost significance" in understanding his thought, because he regarded it as "a public act and an integral part of his moral position."[8] The same can be said of other biographical or semibiographical texts, such as the *Reveries of a Solitary*, which is called by Rousseau an "appendix"

5 Rousseau, *Confessions*, Bk. IX, 379.
6 Jean-Jacques Rousseau, *Correspondance Générale de J.-J. Rousseau*, ed. T. Dufour and P. P. Plan (16 vols.; Paris: Armand Colin, 1924–34), VII, 233. Translated in Masters, *The Political Philosophy of Rousseau*, xiii, 26n.
7 Rousseau, *Confessions*, Bk. IX, 377.
8 Judith N. Shklar, *Men and Citizens: A Study of Rousseau's Social Theory* (Cambridge: Cambridge University Press, 1969), 219.

to the *Confessions*.[9] Many of his private letters are also illuminating.

That Rousseau's own character, temperament, and general attitude toward life are frequently held up by him as representing an ideal is apparent from the texts themselves.
Self-assessments showing his high regard for himself are im-
plicitly or explicitly given in many places: "I . . . believe, and
always have believed, that I am on the whole the best of
men."[10] Even more specifically and categorically, he claims
to be "quite persuaded that of all the men I have known in my
life none was better than myself."[11] He admits having vices
too, but does not quite blame himself for them, since he is
aware that they are "due much more to my situation than to
myself."[12] It is not surprising that a person who takes this
highly favorable view of himself and who, moreover, is so
convinced of his own uniqueness as to believe that nature had
to break the mold when it formed him,[13] should also judge
his private life to be of general interest and worthy of emu-
lation.

Another self-assessment by Rousseau which should be
kept in mind when interpreting *The Social Contract* and other
works is the penetrating recognition that "it is as if my heart
and my brain did not belong to the same person." By the
"heart" he means his "passionate temperament, and lively and
headstrong emotions."[14] In innumerable places he draws a
picture of himself as a person who always wants to act on im-

9 Jean-Jacques Rousseau, *The Reveries of a Solitary*, trans. John Gould Fletcher
    (New York: Lennox Hill, 1971), Bk. I, 39.
10 Rousseau, *Confessions*, Bk. X, 479.
11 Rousseau to Malesherbes, January 4, 1762, in Charles W. Hendel, *Citizen of
    Geneva: Selections from the Letters of Jean-Jacques Rousseau* (New York: Oxford
    University Press, 1937), 206.
12 Rousseau to Malesherbes, January 12, 1762, in Hendel, *Citizen of Geneva*,
    209.
13 See the famous introductory paragraphs of the *Confessions*, Bk. I, 17.
14 Rousseau, *Confessions*, Bk. III, 112–13.

pulse, is moved by his passions, and is frequently engrossed in feelings and imaginings, ranging from pastoral dreaming to pantheistic revery and "dizzy ecstacy." [15] Rousseau's obsessive impatience with everything that tends to restrain his inclinations of the moment is too well known to require elaboration. The tendency is summed up in his statement that "it is hardly in me to subject myself to restraint." [16] In *Emile* the theme of removing checks on man's spontaneous self is developed into a program of education, one principle of which is that "the only habit the child should be allowed to contract is that of having no habits." [17] Inextricably intertwined with this yearning for unbridled freedom is the view that "*man is naturally good*." [18] Rousseau gives this highly instructive key, not only to his personality, but to his philosophy: "I give myself to the impression of the moment without resistance and [even] without scruple; for I am perfectly sure that my heart loves only that which is good. All the evil I ever did in my life was the result of reflection; and the little good I have been able to do was the result of impulse." [19]

The "heart" gives to Rousseau's thinking a pronounced utopian and romantic slant. Radically dissatisfied with society and seemingly constitutionally incapable of coming to terms with it, he is inclined instead to people the world by the help of his "creative imagination" with beings more after his own "heart."

But this tendency to escape from imperfect reality into "an

15 Rousseau to Malesherbes, January 26, 1762, in Hendel, *Citizen of Geneva*, 214.
16 Rousseau, *Confessions*, Bk. IX, 391.
17 Jean-Jacques Rousseau, *Emile*, trans. Barbara Foxley (London: Everyman's Library, 1969), Bk. I, 30.
18 Rousseau, *Correspondence Générale*, XI, 339. Translated in Masters, *The Political Philosophy of Rousseau*, 3 (emphasis in original).
19 Rousseau, *Correspondence Générale*, XVII, 2–3. Translated in Ernst Cassirer, *The Question of Jean-Jacques Rousseau* (Bloomington: Indiana University Press, 1963), 127.

ideal world" believed by Rousseau to be more "worthy of my
exalted feelings"[20] is sometimes checked by moments of so-
briety and realism. Speaking about a period of his life particularly given to romantic revery and worship of nature, he
writes: "However, in the midst of all that, I confess that
sometimes the emptiness of my chimerical dreams suddenly
came to my mind and saddened me."[21] It is striking how
Rousseau's "head," his reason guided by a sense of realism,
will catch up with his "heart" and force qualifications of or
additions to remarks in a more dreamy vein. It revives in him
an awareness of the imperfection of life. In his various writings one comes across perspicacious, piercing, hard-nosed
comments about the human condition remarkably free of the
romantic-utopian slant of the particular work in which they
appear. These flashes of realism, however, are seldom more
than a temporary counterweight to a strong wish to let the
"heart" speak.

An analysis of the romantic-utopian tendency in Rousseau's thought is complicated by the fact that his "heart" does
not always crave the same thing. His works are full of the
glories of an idyllic, pastoral, and anarchic existence, but in
some of them, like the *First Discourse, The Social Contract*,
and *The Government of Poland*, there are also examples of
what may be termed Rousseau's Spartan mood, under whose
influence he extolls the virtues of political discipline, nationalism, and soldierly life. Both inclinations, it should be carefully noted, incorporate a preoccupation with freedom in the
sense of an absence of restraint. The anarchic bent reflects
this propensity in the case of the individual person. The
Spartan bent projects the same yearning onto the collective
level where freedom is invested in the general will, which is
subject to no checks.

For good reasons *The Social Contract* is widely regarded as

20 Rousseau, *Confessions*, Bk. IX, 398.
21 Rousseau to Malesherbes, January 26, 1762, in Hendel, *Citizen of Geneva*,
213.

one of Rousseau's most sober, least romantic works. It does have less of an emotional and impressionistic flavor than some of his other books. Rousseau gives as his intention in *The Social Contract* "to employ solely the power of reason." [22] That remark, however, is not made in any attempt to depreciate the "heart." Since *The Social Contract* is a treatise on political morality, it is important to be aware of Rousseau's reminder that "by reason alone, unaided by conscience, we cannot establish any natural law, and that all natural right is a vain dream if it does not rest upon some instinctive need of the human heart." [23]

Not even *The Social Contract* can be regarded as a treatise of moral and political realism. As will be demonstrated, it is shot through with utopianism. It might perhaps be viewed as representing an effort to fuse the "head" and the "heart," the latter predominantly Spartan in this work. The attempt is closely related to what we may regard as Rousseau's basic purpose in *The Social Contract*: to state the conditions for the re-creation in a social context of the natural goodness and freedom which belongs to man in the state of nature. Reason, Rousseau believes, is not fully developed in that primitive but happy state, but can achieve its true role and potential in civil society under the right circumstances. The problem is to make sure that it does not remain an instrument for the depravity of conventional society, but takes its inspiration from man's true nature. This attempted bringing together of the "head" and "heart," it is interesting to note, cannot be said to involve an ordering principle transcendent of both. A careful reading of *The Social Contract* suggests that there, too, it is the "head" that has to catch up with the "heart" rather than the other way around. The tendency to hide difficulties and blur distinctions, which is largely attributable to Rousseau's utopian bent, is frequently checked but seldom supplanted.

22 Rousseau, *Confessions*, Bk. IX, 378*n*.
23 Rousseau, *Emile*, Bk. IV, 196.

The Rebirth of Nature

VI

In order to put the idea of the general will in the proper context, Rousseau's concept of the state of nature needs to be examined. It is evident that it is central to his political thought and philosophical doctrine in general. In the *First Discourse* Rousseau argues that civilization has degraded and corrupted man. Deeply alienated from society, he identifies with the plight of the descendants of his own century who will beg "Almighty God" to "deliver us from the enlightenment and fatal arts of our forefathers, and give back to us ignorance, innocence, and poverty, the only goods that can give us happiness and are precious in thy sight." [1] This and many other passages in his works raise the much-debated question whether Rousseau wants a return to a primitive, pre-civilized existence. It is doubtful that it can ever be answered with finality. Rousseau himself appears not to have reached a definite conclusion, but wavers depending on his mood and the subject at hand. Especially in certain autobiographical writings he seems to be longing for some sort of pre-societal, anarchic life: "I have never been truly accustomed to civil society where all is worry, obligation, duty, and where my

---

1 Jean-Jacques Rousseau, *The First and Second Discourses*, ed. Roger D. Masters and trans. Roger D. Masters and Judith R. Masters (New York: St. Martin's Press, 1964), First Discourse, 62.

natural independence renders me always incapable of the
subjections necessary to whoever wishes to live amongst
men." [2] But in other places he rules out the possibility of actually returning to a primitive existence. In *Rousseau Judges
Jean-Jacques* he claims to have shown in his works that humanity was happier in this "original state," but he goes on to
say that "human nature does not turn back. Once man has
left it, he can never return to the time of innocence and
equality." [3] Even in *Emile*, which displays more of an individualistic and anarchistic tendency than *The Social Contract*, Rousseau denies that when he sets out to "train a
natural man" he wants to "make him a savage and to send him
back to the woods." [4] But the clearest indication that he does
not envision, or even hope for, a return to pre-societal conditions is the following passage in *The Social Contract* which
expresses his yearning for a new society:

And although in civil society man surrenders some of the advan-
tages that belong to the state of nature, he gains in return far greater
ones; his faculties are so exercised and developed, his mind so en-
larged, his sentiments so ennobled, and his whole spirit so elevated
that, if the abuse of his new condition did not in many cases lower
him to something worse than what he had left, he should constantly
bless the happy hour that lifted him for ever from the state of nature and from a narrow, stupid animal made a creature of intelligence and a man. [5]

Rousseau never makes it entirely clear if he conceives of
the state of nature as an actual historical state, or as an analytical tool, or both. He gives a somewhat different impres-

2 Jean-Jacques Rousseau, *The Reveries of a Solitary*, Bk. VI, 132.
3 Translated in Cassirer, *The Question of Jean-Jacques Rousseau* (Bloomington:
Indiana University Press, 1963), 54.
4 Jean-Jacques Rousseau, *Emile*, Bk. IV, 217.
5 Jean-Jacques Rousseau, *The Social Contract*, trans. Maurice Cranston (Harmondsworth: Penguin Books, 1968), Bk. I, Chap. VIII, 64–65.

sion depending on his line of argument. The ambiguity is apparent in his description of it as "a state which no longer exists, which perhaps never existed, which probably never will exist, and about which it is nevertheless necessary to have precise notions in order to judge our present state correctly." We do not have to resolve the question here. It is certain that, whatever else it is, the state of nature is a normative and analytical concept. In Rousseau's own words, it is employed in an effort of "hypothetical and conditional reasonings better suited to clarify the nature of things than to show their true origin." It is an attempt to isolate that element in human nature which is not the product of the degeneracy of historical society. When he writes about separating "what is original from what is artificial in the present nature of man," he is concerned with distinguishing the depravity of civilized man as he now exists from his true, essential nature by virtue of which he can be said to be happy and good. [6]

Rousseau points to two fundamental driving forces in man in the pre-societal state of innocence. The most important is self-love (*amour de soi*), which is essentially a wish for self-preservation. He differs from Hobbes in believing that "since the state of nature is that in which care of our self-preservation is the least prejudicial to the self-preservation of others, that state was consequently the best suited to peace and the most appropriate for the human race." Rousseau criticizes Hobbes for not having noticed in the state of nature a second "principle": "Pity is a natural sentiment which, moderating in each individual the activity of love of oneself, contributes to the mutual preservation of the entire species. It carries us without reflection to the aid of those whom we see suffer; in the state of nature, it takes the place of laws, morals, and virtue, with the advantage that no one is tempted

6 Rousseau, *The First and Second Discourses* (Second), 93, 103, 92–93.

to disobey its gentle voice." [7] These primordial drives together form the core of man's true nature and are the source of human goodness.

In his quasi-chronological account of the emergence of social life in the *Second Discourse*, Rousseau writes with longing of "man in his primitive state . . . placed by nature at equal distances from the stupidity of brutes and the fatal enlightenment of civil man." This state, he thinks, was the "happiest" and "best for man." "The human race was made to remain in it always," and man "must have come out of it only by some fatal accident, which for the common good ought never to have happened." [8] In this blessed state, man's natural inclinations of self-love and pity made possible both complete individual freedom and independence and a harmonious living together with others, a life of "peaceful anarchy" in Emile Durkheim's phrase. [9] There came a time, however, when because of the pressure of circumstance men started to apply themselves to tasks that a single person could not perform by himself. Individual independence gave way to relations of dependence. "From the moment one man needed the help of another, as soon as they observed that it was useful for a single person to have provisions for two, equality disappeared, property was introduced, labor became necessary." By this process, which created social relations, man's natural freedom was destroyed and "the law of property and inequality" established. [10] Self-love was transformed into selfish love (*amour propre*). Before, under conditions of natural equality and lack of interdependence among men, self-love and pity had combined to produce a benevolent identification with others. Now, aided by the development of reason, awareness

---

7 *Ibid.*, 129, 132–33.
8 *Ibid.*, 150–51.
9 Emile Durkheim, *Montesquieu and Rousseau* (Ann Arbor: University of Michigan Press, 1960), 135.
10 Rousseau, *First and Second Discourses* (Second), 151, 160.

of inequality gives rise to vanity, snobbishness, contempt, and competition. No longer is the individual able to identify with others; he *compares* himself to them.

It is essential to understanding Rousseau's conception of morality to be alert to his associating man's original goodness with a semiconscious communion with nature. My own argument has been that the ethical life is dependent on man's being detached through symbolical thought from his own impulses. Having the ability to judge himself with reference to an independent standard, he has freedom in relation to his own drives. For Rousseau, it should be observed, being detached from oneself in this manner is a sign of depravity. To reflect about one's present condition and to entertain alternative possibilities is to have lost the warm, instinctual immediacy of natural goodness. (Rousseau's line of argument is not without considerable ambiguity, since pity, for instance, would seem to presuppose at least some capacity for self-detachment.) Although man's social awareness cannot be erased once it has appeared, Rousseau's hope is for man somehow to recover his origins.

Existing society thus has perverted man's natural goodness and stifled the natural freedom from which it is indistinguishable. And according to Rousseau human nature does not turn back. What, then, could men hope for? Rousseau is opting in *The Social Contract* for a new type of society and culture. It is to be one of Spartan simplicity and one in the service, not of conventional artificiality and vanity, but, as far as possible, of man's true nature. Cassirer states the problem in this way: "How can we build a genuine and truly human community without falling in the process into the evils and depravity of conventional society?"[11] The goal is to recapture in a social existence, from which there is no escape, man's

11 Cassirer, *The Question of Jean-Jacques Rousseau*, 54.

original goodness, and to inspire social life, including the sciences and the arts, with man's natural inclinations. For Rousseau, Leo Strauss observes, "the good life consists in the closest approximation to the state of nature which is possible on the level of humanity." [12]

The theoretical task of *The Social Contract* is anticipated in the *First Discourse* where Rousseau complains of the lack in contemporary societies of a virtuous devotion to the "fatherland." "We have physicists, geometers, chemists, astronomers, poets, musicians, painters; we no longer have citizens." [13] What is needed is a new type of social cohesion. Rousseau sets out to show in *The Social Contract* how man's natural freedom can be recreated in civil society by attaching each individual to a common goal. "'How to find a form of association which will defend the person and goods of each member with the collective force of all, and under which each individual, while uniting himself with the others, obeys no one but himself, and remains as free as before.' This is the fundamental problem to which the social contract holds the solution." [14] Rousseau claims to have viewed his task in this light: "'What is the nature of the government best fitted to create the most virtuous, the most enlightened, the wisest, and, in fact, the best people, taking the word 'best' in its highest sense?' I believed that I saw a close relationship between that question and another, very nearly though not quite the same: 'What is the government which by its nature always adheres closest to the law?'" [15]

The law, it becomes clear in *The Social Contract*, is the general will, described by Rousseau as a law that a people,

12 Leo Strauss, *Natural Right and History* (Chicago: University of Chicago Press, 1953), 282.
13 Rousseau, *First and Second Discourses* (First), 59.
14 Rousseau, *Social Contract*, Bk. I, Chap. VI, 60.
15 Rousseau, *Confessions*, Bk. IX, 377.

meaning each member, gives to itself. This is the answer to his rhetorical question, "By what inconceivable art has a means been found of making men free by making them subject?" [16]

Equality or Slavery

The analysis of the general will is complicated at almost every turn by the abstract, utopian nature of much of Rousseau's thinking. His proneness to speculate in isolation from concrete reality is illustrated by the conception of slavery which is implied in his famous remark that "man was born free, and he is everywhere in chains." [17]

According to Rousseau's definition, slavery entails "absolute dominion for one party and absolute obedience for the other." It means that "you take away all freedom of the will" from the weaker party. On the basis of this definition, one may ask if there has ever been a genuine case of slavery. Is there in the real world an example of a relationship in which one person has total power over another? The subjugated person, it would seem, never, short of death, completely loses the freedom to defy his oppressor in thought and deed. In the extreme case, he can accept death rather than submission to another will. Where slavery is concerned, the master has got only limited power. If he wants to get any work out of the slave or avoid his hatred, he must be willing to give some consideration to his needs and wishes. In the real world, in other words, there is even in a slave-master relationship an element of "reciprocity" and "mutual obligation," a recognition of

16 Jean-Jacques Rousseau, *A Discourse on Political Economy*, in *The Social Contract and Discourses*, trans. G. D. H. Cole (New York: E. P. Dutton & Co., 1950), 293.
17 Rousseau, *Social Contract*, Bk. I, Chap. I, 49.

"rights," something which Rousseaus rules out by definition: "The words 'slavery' and 'right' are contradictory, they cancel each other out." [18]

The same abstract way of thinking marks Rousseau's criticism of "the right of the strongest." Surely, that principle cannot be the basis for obedience to political authority, he believes. Such authority, if it is to be legitimate, must be based on the free consent of the governed. "Force," he argues, "is a physical power; I do not see how its effects could produce morality. To yield to force is an act of necessity, not of will." [19] We have already questioned the idea that yielding to force is ever a "necessity." Another problem with this statement is Rousseau's artificially narrow conception of what constitutes "force" in human relationships. He ignores such intangible but nevertheless very important sources of power as intelligence, beauty, and charisma. He also ignores the kinds of force which, variously in various societies, are considered ability and which have a direct bearing on people's notion of what constitutes a moral ordering of society. Implied in Rousseau's discussion of right is the idea that all legitimate political authority must rest on abstract egalitarian morality. Right has nothing to do with force, says Rousseau. Morality is what it is regardless of the strengths of disputing or competing individuals.

But Rousseau is discussing the basis for a lawful political order. What about actual legal rights as we know them in society? Are they not, in part at least, the result of a balancing of political power, a result of compromise under the guidance of more or less enlightened self-interest? And are they not largely the result of a recognition of the social value of some kinds of "force"? It would seem that an adjustment to "force,"

18 *Ibid.*, Bk. I, Chap. IV, 55, 58.
19 *Ibid.*, Bk. I, Chap III, 52.

in the expanded sense of strength and ability of various types, is an unavoidable ingredient in all legislation—even in legislation inspired by moral motives. Realistically, morality may be expected in the form of a spirit of magnanimity between men of differing strengths, rooted in a sense of common transcendent purpose. Among those of inferior ability this magnanimity is manifested in the willing recognition of the claims of true superiority; among those of superior ability in the willing reduction of their claims to the well-deserved rewards of their efforts.[20] In his discussion of political right Rousseau simply rules out that laws might derive legitimacy from compromise between men of different "force." For political authority to be acceptable it must rest on egalitarian morality alone. This, he believes, can be achieved through a social contract which is entered into freely on a basis of equality. It substitutes "a moral and lawful equality for whatever physical inequality that nature may have imposed on mankind."[21]

Rousseau defines *right* and *force* in such an unrealistic way that no really legitimate state can be said to have ever existed, and so that the true state he envisions must of necessity be a utopia, an ideal which flies in the face of historical experience. Political legitimacy he views as synonymous with pure morality, as he understands it.

The "head" makes Rousseau admit that even in the state founded on the social contract it is possible that an immoral popular will, the will of all, which is presumably based on mere "force," will sometimes challenge the general will. But the "heart" does not relinquish control. It prevents Rousseau from seeing that as a *practical* matter it may be necessary to

20 See Paul Elmer More, "Justice," in *Aristocracy and Justice*, Vol. IX of *Shelburne Essays* (11 Vols.; New York: Phaeton Press, 1967).
21 Rousseau, *Social Contract*, Bk. I, Chap. IX, 68.

give some political recognition to what he dismisses as the will of all. He assumes the existence of a popular will which is an expression of pure egalitarian morality, and as such it alone deserves any consideration. I have argued that no civilized state can be built on motives of mere selfishness, however sophisticated. Yet, given human nature as it is known in real life, it appears inescapable that a balancing of conflicting interests will always be a fundamental need in politics. Rousseau is relieved by his utopian frame of mind from confronting and dealing with this important issue. The choice for him is clear-cut: equality or slavery.

Social Freedom

But a utopian slant does not automatically render an idea in political philosophy worthless. It may still offer a valid standard for judging imperfect reality and thus a sound inspiration for political change. We need to decide whether Rousseau's concept of the general will falls in that category.

The general will is the result of an act of association in which each individual voluntarily gives up his natural freedom. The articles of association, Rousseau writes, "are reducible to a single one, namely the total alienation by each associate of himself and all his rights to the whole community." Rousseau is emphatic in his point that "every individual gives himself absolutely" so that he can no longer claim any rights whatever. Through the social contract his rights are transferred to the collective as epitomized in the general will. The latter becomes the inalienable and indivisible sovereign. Rousseau speaks of the appearance of "an artificial and collective body" which "acquires its unity, its common *ego* [*moi commun*], its life and its will." [22] He calls this organism, "re-

22 *Ibid.*, Bk. I, Chap. VI, 60–61.

sembling that of man," [23] "the public person." [24] It is "a moral being possessed of a will; and this general will, which tends always to the preservation and welfare of the whole and of every part, and is the source of the laws, constitutes for all members of the State, in their relations to one another and to it, the rule of what is just or unjust." [25] By participation in this will the individual attains social freedom. "The public person," Rousseau contends, is completely free, for "it would be against the very nature of a political body for the sovereign to set over itself a law which it could not infringe." [26] The sovereign is itself the law.

Through the ingenious postulation of a "public person," made up of each of the citizens and governed by a will which is by definition moral and free, Rousseau has recreated in a social cast the natural freedom which man has lost in conventional society. It should be noted that in his international relations each "public person" is in the state of nature. [27] By his participation in the collective will of the people, the individual is totally subjugated to a unifying political authority, but he is at the same time his own master, for the general will grows out of a will in each person, and "obedience to a law one prescribes to oneself is freedom." [28] The individual need not fear a misuse of power by the sovereign, for a body cannot wish to injure one of its own members.

In the civil society which is established by the social contract, Rousseau argues, human actions become guided by justice and acquire "the moral quality" they did not have in the state of nature. Where before man was ruled by mere in-

23 Rousseau, *Political Economy*, 289.
24 Rousseau, *Social Contract*, Bk. I, Chap. VI, 61.
25 Rousseau, *Political Economy*, 289–90.
26 Rousseau, *Social Contract*, Bk. I, Chap. VII, 62.
27 Rousseau, *Political Economy*, 290.
28 Rousseau, *Social Contract*, Bk. I, Chap. VIII, 65.

stincts, primary among them self-love and pity, he now has the use of the developed faculties of man as a creature of society, including reason. These together make for a social consciousness previously lacking. Through the social contract, so we may interpret Rousseau's thinking, these faculties are put at the disposal of man's natural inclinations to produce a general elevation of the spirit. There appears a sense of duty and right. In the words of John Charvet, "The new social consciousness is founded on nature, but at the same time completes it." [29]

It should be injected that also in *The Social Contract* Rousseau is vacillating between a chronological and an abstract conceptual analysis, without ever removing the ambiguity. In his discussion of the social contract he claims to be speaking of "the passing from the state of nature to the civil society." [30] Yet, he is positing that the contracting individuals already possess the social consciousness which is also alleged to be the result of a social existence.

What is it about the social contract that makes it possible to avoid the degeneration that has afflicted historical societies? A crucial factor is that it is based on equality: "The social pact, far from destroying natural equality, substitutes, on the contrary, a moral and lawful equality for whatever physical inequality that nature may have imposed on mankind; so that however unequal in strength and intelligence, men become equal by covenant and by right." [31]

It will be remembered that according to Rousseau it was the appearance of inequality through the idea of property that gave rise to the perversion of natural self-love into vanity and

---

29 John Charvet, "Individual Identity and Social Consciousness in Rousseau's Philosophy," in Maurice Cranston and Richard S. Peters (eds.), *Hobbes and Rousseau* (Garden City: Anchor Books, 1972), 476.
30 Rousseau, *Social Contract*, Bk. I, Chap. VIII, 64.
31 *Ibid.*, Bk. I, Chap. IX, 68.

other kinds of depravity. These are symptomatic of a lack of identification with others. This may be avoided in society, Rousseau believes, by creating the circumstances under which self-love, which is "always good, always in accordance with the order of nature," can come into its own again. "Extend self-love to others and it is transformed into virtue, a virtue which has its root in the heart of every one of us."[32] Under the social contract, self-love becomes a powerful moral force, for the citizens "all pledge themselves under the same conditions and must all enjoy the same rights."[33] These conditions of equality, ruling out corrupting relations of dependence, make possible the identification of each citizen with all others. Together with natural pity, so we may interpret Rousseau's meaning, self-love inspires a strong sense of social belonging. This new type of identification, which is made possible by the development of man's faculties and associated by Rousseau with morality, can be said to be "founded on nature insofar as the love of others follows from and is a completion of one's natural self-love (*amour de soi*)."[34]

It is important for the proper understanding of the general will to be aware of the role that Rousseau ascribes to self-love. The love of mankind is "nothing but the love of justice within us," he points out in *Emile*. This love of justice, let it be carefully noted, is rooted in man's primordial instincts. In an illuminating footnote essential to grasping Rousseau's conception of morality, he writes: "The love of others, springing from self-love, is the source of human justice."[35] The same idea is expressed in *The Social Contract*: "How should it be that the general will is always rightful and that all men

32 Rousseau, *Emile*, Bk. IV, 174, 215.
33 Rousseau, *Social Contract*, Bk. II, Chap. IV, 76.
34 Charvet, "Individual Identity and Social Consciousness in Rousseau's Philosophy," 478.
35 Rousseau, *Emile*, Bk. IV, 215, 197n.

constantly wish the happiness of each but for the fact that
there is no one who does not take that word 'each' to pertain
to himself and in voting for all think of himself?" [36] Morality,
in other words, is a social version of private self-love by way
of an identification with others. When one remembers that
self-love in the state of nature is essentially a wish for physical self-preservation, it is not surprising to find that in several
places in *The Social Contract* and elsewhere Rousseau formulates the goal of the state in terms of mutual protection. If
you look for the motives which make men unite themselves in
civil societies, "you will find no other motive than that of assuring the property, life, and liberty of each member by the
protection of all." [37] We shall return, however, to the moral
implications of his notion of self-love.

While there is abundant evidence for viewing the general
will as a collective, "extended" version of man's natural inclinations, it is clear that it is not simply some enlargement of
self-love and pity as they appear in the state of nature. The
general will emerges in a social context, where man has been
transformed form a "narrow, stupid animal" into a "creature
of intelligence and a man." It benefits from conditions under
which man's different faculties are "exercised and developed." [38] We may view the general will as the result of
putting these faculties at the disposal of man's true nature.
Deriving their propelling force from man's original inclinations, they are rescued from becoming the tools of degeneracy
and instead become constitutive elements of a wholly moral
political will. Not only does the general will occur in a social
environment, it speaks about social problems. Projected
through the prism of social life, man's original inclination

36 Rousseau, *Social Contract*, Bk. II, Chap. IV, 75.
37 Rousseau, *Political Economy*, 293.
38 Rousseau, *Social Contract*, Bk. I, Chap. VIII, 65.

towards what is good is applied to a whole new range of concerns and possibilities. To Rousseau falls the task of showing what is conduct according to nature under these circumstances.

The General Will

It is assumed by Rousseau that the general will is not some sectional, particularistic, arbitrary expression of opinion. On the contrary, it is the very principle by which morality is defined. In spite of that, Rousseau frequently speaks of the general will as a mere aggregation or harmony of "private interests." "It is what is common to those different interests which yields the social bond; if there were no point on which separate interests coincided, then society could not conceivably exist. And it is precisely on the basis of this common interest that society must be governed." [1]

Speaking of the "individual desires" of the citizens, Rousseau asserts that "if we take away from these same wills, the pluses and minuses which cancel each other out, the sum of the difference is the general will." The same emphasis on numbers marks his contention that for the general will to be truly general "all the votes must be counted." Referring to the proposals of the lawgiver, but laying down a general principle, Rousseau maintains that "there can be no assurance that an individual will is in conformity with the general will until it has submitted to the free suffrage of the people." In another context he states without equivocation: "Any law

---

1 Jean-Jacques Rousseau, *The Social Contract*, trans. Maurice Cranston (Harmondsworth: Penguin Books, 1968), Bk. II, Chap. I, 69.

which the people has not ratified in person is void; it is not law at all." The clear implication is that the general will does not exist apart from an actual vote in the popular assembly. The element of egalitarian individualism in Rousseau's thought becomes even more evident in his example of the state with ten thousand citizens. In this state, he argues, each person has got only a "ten-thousandth part of the sovereign authority." [2] These and similar statements in *The Social Contract* and other works would seem to indicate that the general will results from some sort of canceling out of extreme or abnormal opinions and an addition of the remaining private interests of the citizens. But if the general will is transcendent of all particular wills, one may ask, why all this talk of private interests, numbers, and ratifications in person?

While it is evident that there is a strong connection between Rousseau's egalitarian individualism and his idea of the general will, he concedes that absolute authority cannot be claimed for just any numerical majority. It should be clear, he writes, that "the general will derives its generality less from the number of voices than from the common interest which unites them." And although he never develops the idea with consistency and clarity, he hints at a basic opposition between private interests and the general will in his distinction of the latter from the will of all: "The general will studies only the common interest while the will of all studies private interest, and is indeed no more than the sum of individual desires." [3] This passage, however, is immediately followed by the sentence previously quoted, which describes the general will as the result of a process of canceling out and addition of particular wills.

2 *Ibid.*, Bk. II, Chap. III, 72–73; Bk. II, Chap. II, 70*n*.; Bk. II, Chap. VII, 86; Bk. III, Chap. XV, 141; Bk. III, Chap. I, 103.
3 *Ibid.*, Bk. II, Chap. IV, 76; Bk. II, Chap. III, 72.

Rousseau is trying, on the one hand, to present the general will as an absolute standard and, on the other hand, to make it somehow dependent on the assent of the individual as a separate entity. The closest he comes to joining these two perspectives, it may be gathered from his partially contradictory statements, is the belief that under certain circumstances majority assent serves to confirm a will that is somehow latent in the people, but actually manifested as the general will only in a vote by the popular assembly. Such a rendering of his thought does not remove, but only restates, the basic ambiguity.

One important cause of Rousseau's difficulty is that he does not conceive of man as by nature a social being. Man by himself, he believes, "is entirely complete and solitary." The general will, therefore, could not be the structuring principle of man's essential nature. It must be some kind of addition, extension, or merging of individuality. Man's social nature has to be *created* from this core. Rousseau writes: "The constitution of a man is the work of nature; that of the state is the work of artifice." [4] Elaborating on this theme, he argues:

If it is good to know how to deal with men as they are, it is much better to make them what there is need that they should be. The most absolute authority is that which penetrates into a man's inmost being, and concerns itself no less with his will than with his actions. It is certain that all peoples become in the long run what the government makes them. . . . Make men, therefore, if you would command men: if you would have them obedient to the laws, make them love the laws, and then they will need only to know what is their duty to do it. [5]

The general will, we are forced to believe, is not a preexist-

4 *Ibid.*, Bk. II, Chap. VII, 84; Bk. III, Chap. XI, 135.
5 Jean-Jacques Rousseau, *A Discourse on Political Economy*, in *The Social Contract and Discourses*, trans. G. D. H. Cole (New York: E. P. Dutton & Co., 1950), 297–98.

ing, universal principle or even a sense of political direction somehow derived from such a principle, but a standard that is made. As Rousseau says in *The Social Contract*, it is a law that man gives himself. What rescues Rousseau from the accusation of complete arbitrariness is his attempt to base the general will on what is good by nature. It has moral authority, he believes, because it springs from the individual's original inclinations.

The General Will and Representation

One of the most noteworthy elements of Rousseau's argument in *The Social Contract* is the sharp distinction between the legislative and executive function in the state. According to him all legislative authority belongs to the general will which "must be general in its purpose as well as in its nature" and "should spring from all and apply to all." The general will "cannot relate to any particular object." [6] The application of general rules to specific cases falls to the executive power, which Rousseau variously calls the government, the magistrates, or the prince. The executive function is completely subject to the sovereign general will. While the legislative power must be exercised in a democratic fashion with all the citizens participating in the vote, executive decisions can be entrusted, depending on the circumstances, to a single magistrate, which Rousseau calls monarchy, just a few, which he names aristocracy, or all of the citizens in person, which is what he means by democracy. Rousseau's insistence on a sharp distinction between the executive and legislative, it may be argued, is symptomatic of a basic philosophical confusion involving an attempt to set up as absolute a political

6 Rousseau, *Social Contract*, Bk. II, Chap. IV, 75; Bk. II, Chap. VI, 81.

standard which is in fact much less than universal. We may expose some of that confusion by analyzing his view of representation.

As far as the legislative function is concerned Rousseau flatly rejects the idea of representation. It is ruled out by the very nature of the general will. "Sovereignty cannot be represented, for the same reason that it cannot be alienated; its essence is the general will, and will cannot be represented—either it is the general will or it is something else." And he goes on to say: "Since the law is nothing other than a declaration of the general will, it is clear that there cannot be representation of the people in the legislative power." In a revealing illustration of his meaning Rousseau disputes the claim of the English people to be free. In reality, he points out, it is free only when it elects members of the Parliament. "As soon as the Members are elected, the people is enslaved." [7]

Rousseau's hostility to representation is further evidence of the view that the general will is inseparable from actual popular decisions. If it did transcend them and could be known by men individually, there would be a possibility of legislators representing the citizenry. Having ruled this out, Rousseau still does not face the problem that every single person can hardly be present for every vote in the assembly. Also, those who are yet too young to be members will be affected by laws that are passed by it. If this apparent violation of Rousseau's rule that laws must "spring from all and apply to all" [8] is not to nullify all actual legislation, it would seem that those not participating in the vote must somehow be represented by those present in the assembly.

Curiously, Rousseau drops his emphatic opposition to representation in his discussion of the executive function of the

7 *Ibid.*, Bk. III, Chap. XV, 141, 142, 141.
8 *Ibid.*, Bk. II, Chap. IV, 75.

state: "There may and should be such representation in the
executive power, which is only the instrument for applying
the law." [9] To understand the importance in Rousseau's
thought of the distinction between legislative and executive
we need to look closer at his idea of general laws and particular applications.

Rousseau's notion of general laws, *i.e.*, of manifestations
of the general will, is extremely difficult to pin down. The
reason is the tension produced in his thought by his attempt
to join together to the point of identification what cannot be
joined completely, if at all, namely the absolute standard of
morality, on the one hand, and expressions of political will,
on the other. Vaguely aware that the ultimate principle of
right and wrong cannot simply be identified with specific
political acts, but at the same time anxious to present the will
of the majority as the final standard of morality, he is led to
conceive of the laws passed by the general will in a highly
abstract manner. For a legislative act to be truly a law, Rousseau argues, the matter it deals with must be "as general as
the will which makes it." The idea is explained further in his
statement that "every act of sovereignty, that is, every au-
thentic act of the general will, binds or favours all the citizens equally, so that the sovereign recognizes only the whole
body of the nation and makes no distinction between any of
the members who compose it." As if this standard were not
difficult enough to apply to real political life, he points out
that "the law considers all subjects collectively and all actions
in the abstract." Negatively stated, the general will "loses its
natural rectitude when it is directed towards any particular
and circumscribed object." [10]

9 *Ibid.*, Bk. III, Chap. XV, 142.
10 *Ibid.*, Bk. II, Chap. VI, 81; Bk. II, Chap. IV, 76; Bk. II, Chap. VI, 82; Bk. II,
    Chap. IV, 75.

It may be asked what a law would be like which does not favor or disfavor any citizen, but deals identically with all of them. It should be noted that Rousseau is not just talking about a law that is inspired by a selfless, sincere commitment to the common good, but about one that actually "binds or favours all the citizens equally." Can such a piece of legislation be imagined? Barring the postulation of complete equality, including removal of all individual uniqueness and differences of circumstance, it would seem to be impossible. Not surprisingly, whenever Rousseau offers concrete examples of genuine laws, he appears to compromise his principle of generality rather severely.

According to Rousseau, the sovereign does not have the right to "impose greater burdens on one subject than on another."[11] That would seem to rule out even broadly formulated laws of the type that "all able-bodied men shall be liable to induction into military service," or that "all shall be taxed according to a certain rate." Clearly, even such laws would be more of a burden on some people than on others. Still, in regard to taxes Rousseau lays down the basic rule that they should depend on "a general will, decided by vote of a majority, and on the basis of a proportional rating which leaves nothing arbitrary in the imposition of the tax."[12] Whether arbitrary or not, it is anything but self-evident that the principle of proportionality affects "all the citizens equally." Indeed, it is difficult to see how any one rate of taxation could accomplish this goal. It is worthy of note that Rousseau even gives his support to the idea of taxes as a "fine." Heavy taxes should be laid, he thinks, "on all that multiplicity of objects

11 *Ibid.*, Bk. II, Chap. IV, 77.
12 Rousseau, *Political Economy*, 320. In *The Social Contract* Rousseau has some reservations about taxation, preferring instead "compulsory service." Bk. III, Chap. XV, 140.

of luxury, amusement, and idleness, which strike the eyes of all." [13] Although it is not entirely clear whether he regards punitive taxes as a matter of legislation or just an executive application of legislative authority, the example only makes explicit the unavoidable element of discrimination in all actual laws. So long as no two individuals are identical and live under identical circumstances, laws, however "general" in formulation, will affect them differently. Not only that, no two members of a popular assembly will be able to conceive of the meaning and consequences of a proposed law in the same way. Generality in the strict sense is threatened from both directions.

In a discussion of actual pieces of legislation Rousseau cannot but infuse his concept of generality with various kinds of particularity. By definition, a civil law cannot affect all equally. It discriminates in favor of a certain state of affairs. To speak of a law without any bias for or against individuals or groups is to speak of a pure abstraction, which does not become any more meaningful because allegedly a manifestation of pure morality. In its implied disregard for the uniqueness of individuals and circumstances, Rousseau's notion of the generality of law calls to mind Kant's famous ethical rule that we should always act in such a way that the principle of our action could become the standard for universal legislation. Both have a disembodied quality growing out of abstract egalitarian assumptions at odds with infinitely diverse human reality. They reduce man to a ficticious common denominator.

I am arguing, then, that all legislation is adjusted to special circumstances and directed towards a specific end. A political law must of necessity exhibit the characteristic which Rous-

13 Rousseau, *Political Economy*, 328.

seau contends will destroy its "natural rectitude," namely be directed towards a "particular and circumscribed object." When Rousseau writes, for instance, that some laws in the state will have to be designed specifically to meet the needs of a certain country, he is revealing an element of particularity which is necessarily present in some form, not only in every law, but in every human act. The generality of law, in other words, is not a distinct philosophical category, but a theoretical fiction, a convenient pragmatic classification at best.

But if legislation has in it always a measure of particularity and application to special circumstances, it cannot be sharply distinguished from executive acts. The philosophical artificiality of this division becomes the more apparent the more one considers concrete examples. Take, for instance, a popular assembly which appropriates money for some public project. Is it exercising legislative authority, or has it assumed an executive function? Needless to say, one could give examples of decisions with more of a "legislative" slant and less of an "executive" slant, and vice versa. The point is that it would not involve a jump from one philosophically distinct category of political action to another, but only movement along a sliding scale.

Rousseau's purpose is to establish the absolute authority of the general will of the people. To accomplish that he feels the need to keep it untainted by all arbitrariness and particularism. He is sufficiently under the influence of the classical and Judaeo-Christian tradition not to make an easy identification of pure morality, even as he understands it, with specific political acts. He suggests a fundamental difference between the general will as such and the multiplicity of particular applications. Hence his distinction between the sovereign and the "government." "Executive power cannot belong to the generality of the people as legislative or sovereign,

since executive power is exercised only in particular acts
which are outside the province of law and therefore outside
the province of the sovereign which can act only to make
laws." [14] The introduction of this distinction places Rousseau
in an impossible position. In so far as he wants to preserve
the generality, and thus the morality, of the general will, he
is forced to make of it a meaningless abstraction, and in so far
as he wants to present it as a real, positive force in politics
dealing with concrete matters, it loses its generality.

Rousseau is not satisfied, as are Plato and Aristotle and
their Christian counterparts, with envisioning the possibility
of politics as *participation* in the ethical purpose of life. He
wants morality to be manifested to the full in the state, in the
sovereign people. The theoretical result, his notion of the
general will, must be regarded as an adulteration of the
genuine standard of morality, as the absolutization of a political principle that is far from universal. If a law is truly general in the strict sense of transcending all particular circumstances, it cannot also be a civil law or a political will, be
it legislative, however "general," or an executive application
of legislative authority; and if it is a manifestation of immanent reality, it is that much less than universal and absolute.
Rousseau's wish to invest the collective will of the people with
unlimited authority and freedom prevents him from seeing
that with reference to the real standard of morality both legislative and executive acts could only be imperfect applications
to particular circumstances. Proceeding on the premise that
man is naturally good, neither is he held back by a recognition that the ability of the state to play a moral role is severely
circumscribed by the inherent weakness of human nature.

Rousseau's hostility to the idea of representation is not only
directed against the narrowly political concept. It derives

14 Rousseau, *Social Contract*, Bk. III, Chap. I, 101.

from his unwillingness to accept an ethical principle which might restrain political authority and leave men an appeal beyond the decisions of the state. As will be discussed further, his notion of morality in *The Social Contract* is indistinguishable from a wish to secure the complete unity of the political order. This unity would be threatened by the admission that politics is at best only an attempt to *represent* a standard above all particular societies and particular wills. The moral authority of the state, he thinks, must be under no suspicion.

The Rejection of Constitutionalism

The same unwillingness to place politics under a higher law is reflected in Rousseau's emphatic denunciation of constitutionalism. "The supreme authority can no more be modified than it can be alienated; to limit it is to destroy it. It is absurd and self-contradictory that the sovereign should give itself a superior." Using the analogy of an individual person, he asserts that "it is absurd that anyone should wish to bind himself for the future." The same holds true for an entire state: "It would be against the very nature of a political body for the sovereign to set over itself a law which it could not infringe." Rousseau's usual abhorrence of constraint translates into the idea that the people should always be completely free to alter its laws. "Yesterday's law is not binding today," he writes. He even goes so far as to say that if the people chooses "to do itself an injury, who has the right to prevent it from doing so?" [15] So concerned is he with laying down the absolute freedom of the sovereign, he forgets having already defined the general will in such a way that it could not yield an injurious decision.

15 *Ibid.*, Bk. III, Chap. XVI, 144; Bk. II, Chap. I, 70; Bk. I, Chap. VII, 62; Bk. III, Chap. XI, 135; Bk. II, Chap. XII, 99.

According to Rousseau, it is an advantage from the stand-point of securing respect for laws if they acquire the dignity of age. Still, constitutional rules which cannot be as easily changed as other laws are expressly forbidden. Setting down what would appear ironically to be a more rigid and funda-mental provision than any constitutional requirement, he proclaims that at the opening of each assembly the people must be asked if it pleases them to maintain the present form of government. "There is not in the state any fundamental law which may not be revoked, not even the social pact." [16] It is difficult not to suspect a strong connection between this view and Rousseau's pervasive autobiographical theme, "I love liberty; I hate embarrassment, worry, and constraint." [17]

We have already noted that there is in Rousseau's thinking a pronounced majoritarian tendency. What is right, he claims, becomes revealed by majority vote, provided that those voting be properly informed about the issue at hand, that they make up their own minds, and are not affected by any sectional interests. When the majority has spoken, the minority cannot legitimately persist in its views and try to convert the majority, for it has now been proven wrong. Pre-sumably, it should immediately give up its mistaken, selfish opinions. Indeed, since there is in politics only a wholly right and a wholly wrong, there would seem to be no reason why the state should tolerate opposition. In view of Rousseau's prohibition against all "sectional associations," it is difficult to see how any effective, organized opposition *could* exist.

Rousseau makes no allowance for the possibility that even under the most favorable conditions of abundant information and public-spiritedness the majority might only imperfectly express the general will. That recognition would point to the

16 *Ibid.*, Bk. III, Chap. XVIII, 148.
17 Rousseau, *Confessions*, Bk. I, 46.

need for constitutional provisions designed to bring out the best in its opinions and restrain what is not worthy of public implementation. But Rousseau does not, and *cannot* if he is to preserve his concept of the general will, concede the existence of any political shades or nuances. "Either the will is general or it is not." [18] Differences of opinion in the state must fall in a black-and-white category.

Rousseau's sense of realism does interfere with the easy flow of his thought. He admits that in practice the majority may not always be right. By inference, the minority is not always wrong. In the face of the danger that the will of all dethrone the rightful popular will, one might expect that Rousseau would give at least some serious thought to placing constitutional restrictions on the freedom of the momentary majority. If the general will does indeed express the permanent, common interest of the people, it would seem that its public implementation would not be hurt by having the wishes of the majority filtered through a system of institutional checks by means of which they could prove their quality as the enduring popular will. It would appear logical that Rousseau should also lay down some practical guidelines for restraining a powerful minority, which, claiming to speak for the general will, might try to usurp the role of the majority. But he speaks only of an "obligation on the minority to accept the decision of the majority." [19] That, in the absence of any constitutional guarantees supported by a tradition of constitutional morality, is scant protection against the possibility of tyranny.

We may cite some further examples in Rousseau's thinking of a seemingly inexorable movement in the direction of constitutionalism which is never completed but suddenly re-

18 Rousseau, *Social Contract*, Bk. II, Chap. II, 70.
19 *Ibid.*, Bk. I, Chap. V, 59.

versed. "By themselves the people always will what is good, but by themselves they do not always discern it," Rousseau writes. He also speaks of the people as a "blind multitude." This assessment would seem to point directly towards putting some legal checks on their will and having popular representatives articulate their interests. But these rather deprecating remarks describe the people only prior to achieving its "fullest strength" through the temporary guidance of the lawgiver. But even after this "enlightenment," Rousseau anticipates some difficulties. He is deeply concerned about the danger that the executive might usurp the authority of the sovereign. To protect against such abuse, Rousseau prescribes "fixed and periodic assemblies which nothing can abolish or prorogue." Although this and other institutional provisions in *The Social Contract* would appear to be unconditional and more fundamental than any law, they are never coupled with suggestions for constitutional protection of the arrangements in question. Not even the laws provided by the lawgiver, which found the new political order, are to receive any such sanction. In a passage which brings Rousseau perilously close to the forbidden idea, he writes: "It is true that . . . one should never touch an established government unless it has become incompatible with the public welfare." As though aware of the constitutional implications of this position, Rousseau hastens to add that "such circumspection is a precept of politics and not a rule of law."[20] Nothing must stop the people from making whatever changes it wants at any time. Significantly, Rousseau is assuming that it would never occur to the citizens of the new state to protect the general will against the immoral will of all by means of constitutional rules. Apparently the sovereign needs and wants complete

20 *Ibid.*, Bk. II, Chap. VI, 83; Bk. III, Chap. XIII, 137; Bk. III, Chap. XVIII, 147.

freedom of movement. Even an attempt to restrain illegitimate political wishes would dangerously circumscribe the ability of the general will to manifest itself.

To the extent that there lingers in Rousseau's thought echoes of the old Western dualistic view of human nature with its rather pessimistic assessment of man's capacity to rise above his lower inclinations, he is pushed in the direction of accepting some form of constitutionalism. But always the basic utopian thrust of his thinking reasserts itself. Inspired by his "heart," he takes it for granted that *somehow*, without any constitutional guarantees, the institutional arrangements which he prescribes will not only be established but respected in the long run by the people. Somehow, the general will is actually going to be expressed by the majority. This assumption goes contrary to what Rousseau himself recognizes as the historical record. It is little more than a hope. Indeed, the importance that Rousseau ascribes to propaganda and other forms of molding public opinion indicates that even in the state based on the social contract the articulation of the general will is not going to be automatic.[21]

The Spontaneity of the Moral Will

Rousseau's refusal in spite of the mentioned complications to subject the will of the majority to any form of restraint is finally explained by his belief that what is good in man is manifested spontaneously. The problem with which he deals in *The Social Contract* is how the circumstances can be

21 See Rousseau's discussion of the fourth kind of law in *The Social Contract*, Bk. II, Chap. XII and Bk. IV, Chap. VIII. The need for propaganda and careful supervision of public opinion is discussed also in *Politics and the Arts: Letter to D'Alembert on the Theatre*, trans. Allan Bloom (Ithaca: Cornell University Press, 1968) and in *The Government of Poland*, trans. Willmoore Kendall (New York: Bobbs-Merrill Co., 1972).

created under which this impulsive goodness will be released. Man needs to be liberated from all artificial motives which pervert and imprison his true nature. Wherever necessary, he must "be forced to be free." [22] But while constraint may sometimes be required to unfetter man's natural inclinations, no limits must be put on that spontaneity once it has been restored to its rightful place as the guide of human behavior.

Such terms as *impulse* and *spontaneity* should not be misunderstood. As applied to Rousseau's moral theory they are not intended to signify irregular bursts of desire and passion or states of directionless effervescence. Rousseau is assuming that in the truly free individual who has thrown off the shackles of traditional civilization, action flows without interruption in a certain beneficial direction. Genuinely spontaneous man is put on a steady course of virtue. This makes him a person of simple desires and needs. His life-style and general demeanor may perhaps even strike the members of corrupt civilization as ascetic. What needs to be understood in particular is that the kind of ordering or regulation which is necessary in a society is viewed by Rousseau as inherent in genuine spontaneity itself. Traditional civilization has ruined this gift of "nature."

According to Rousseau, the citizen who is to vote in the assembly should "make up his own mind for himself [*n'opine que d'après lui*]." [23] We may interpret this to mean in part that he should shut himself out from all alien influences and listen only to his own heart. Open to his natural inclinations, he is in a position to respond morally to the issues that are put to him. The general will, adding or merging the spontaneous wish of all individuals so inspired, thus becomes directed towards what is good by nature.

22 Rousseau, *Social Contract*, Bk. I, Chap. VII, 64.
23 *Ibid.*, Bk. II, Chap. III, 73.

The notion that political morality is incompatible with external influences on the decisions of the individual establishes a link with Rousseau's conception of human innocence in the state of nature. The latter type of goodness is also described as ruined by detachment from the immediacy of one's own drives. In the new social man impulses have been greatly broadened and carry political intentions, but morality is made possible in a corresponding fashion by removal of influences which would make for self-detachment. Critical examination of emerging popular wishes, as encouraged by constitutional checks on the majority of the moment, would sever the bond with the inspirational momentum of nature. The kind of deliberation in the popular assembly which Rousseau endorses and which is ideally very short does not have the purpose of subjecting a previous expression of popular will to scrutiny, but is the way of letting nature find its course in its new, political context.

The view that man's first impulse is good is affirmed over and over again in Rousseau's writings. One of his most appreciative commentators, Ernst Cassirer, observes: "Even the ethical conscience remained for Rousseau a kind of 'instinct'—for it is not based simply upon reflective cogitation but springs from a spontaneous impulse."[24] In *Emile* Rousseau writes that "the first impulses of the heart give rise to the first stirrings of conscience." He goes on to say that "justice and kindness are no mere abstract terms, no mere moral conceptions framed by the understanding, but true affections of the heart enlightened by reason, the natural outcome of our primitive affections."[25] His belief in the spontaneous

24 Ernst Cassirer, *The Question of Jean-Jacques Rousseau* (Bloomington: Indiana University Press, 1963), 109.
25 Jean-Jacques Rousseau, *Emile*, trans. Barbara Foxley (London: Everyman's Library, 1969), Bk. IV, 196.

goodness of man is evidenced also in his autobiographical writings: "I am perfectly sure that my heart loves only that which is good. All the evil I ever did in my life was the result of reflection; and the little good I have been able to do was the result of impulse."[26] The examples of his identification of morality with spontaneity, and of vice with constraint and second thoughts, could be multiplied. This is hardly surprising. If one believes, as Rousseau does, that man is good by nature and evil somehow alien to his essential being, it is only logical to believe that what issues forth from man without the interference of moderating prejudice or reflection is also good.

According to a principle of civil law which Rousseau cites, "no man is bound by a contract with himself." Expanding on this idea, he puts it down as "absurd that anyone should wish to bind himself for the future."[27] Using his notion of the state as a public person, he insists that neither can the state be bound by any promises to itself, such as constitutional laws. We are confronted here by a basic flaw in Rousseau's political philosophy. Is it really true that a person is not bound by a contract with himself? It is of course always possible for an individual simply to disregard such a promise. The ability to do so, however, does not change the fact that he might be *morally* bound to respect it. Do we not repeatedly make promises of that kind? Contrary to Rousseau's ideal for both individual and collective life, it would seem that we are continuously binding ourselves for the future. Our steadiness as moral beings is largely the result of personal commitments to behave or not to behave in a certain fashion. "I shall not again act in that way!" "I will be intellectually honest." "I

26 Jean-Jacques Rousseau, *Correspondence Générale*, XVII, 2–3. Translated in Cassirer, *The Question of Jean-Jacques Rousseau*, 127.
27 Rousseau, *Social Contract*, Bk. I, Chap. VIII, 62; Bk. II, Chap. I, 70.

have to restrain my selfishness." Although in a sense free to disregard such promises to ourselves, we are often morally obligated to respect them. The result of abrogating them is ethical self-condemnation. In an analogous way, is it not possible for the people to make promises to itself, for instance in the form of a constitution, which it is morally obligated to respect?

Under the philosophical theory I have previously developed, respect for promises in furtherance of the goal known in ethical conscience are a *necessity*, if man is to become a reasonably moral being. He will not spontaneously move in that direction. On the contrary, he needs to put checks on his inclination to act selfishly and arbitrarily. Morality is bought at the price of often difficult self-discipline. Rousseau, by contrast, postulates the ontological unity and goodness of human nature. Man divided against himself is for him not an irrevocable fact of human life but a crime perpetrated against man by conventional society.

It should be remembered in this context that when Rousseau talks about virtue and justice he is referring to something rooted in self-love (*amour de soi*). The latter phrase in itself does not invalidate his ethical standard. The "self" in question might conceivably be, not some egotistical will, but a moral principle known by man and at the same time transcendent of him. Such a dualistic conception of human nature, however, is in sharp contradiction to Rousseau's philosophy. His rejection of such a view may be illustrated by this important passage, quoted in part before, which takes one to the very center of his ethical thought:

If the enthusiasm of an overflowing heart identifies me with my fellow-creature, if I feel so to speak, that I will not let him suffer lest I should suffer too, I care for him because I care for myself, and the reason of the precept is found in nature herself, which inspires

me with the desire for my own welfare wherever I may be. From
this I conclude that it is false to say that the precepts of natural law
are based on reason only; they have a firmer and more solid foundation. The love of others, springing from self-love, is the source of
human justice.[28]

All morality is thus derived from a concern for the private
ego. There is in this illuminating statement not even a hint to
the tension in man between a higher and lower self. There is
no recognition that love belongs properly only to that in ourselves and others which has ethical worth, not to the whole of
man but to our potential for spiritual growth. Rousseau is describing a gush of indiscriminate sympathy. He sees no need
to ask whether the self from which it emanates and the self
with which the bearer identifies in the other person is morally uplifting or degrading. It is quite possible, for instance,
to sympathize with the wish of a criminal to escape from a
prison or the wish of a drug addict to get a shot of narcotics,
but normally such feelings of pity would have nothing to do
with morality. They actually stem from and attach to a self
which is contrary to the higher good. Unwilling to accept
moral depravity as an inherent human characteristic, Rousseau does not recognize the urgent need to discriminate between various inclinations of the "heart." His view of human
nature is monistic, and he regards morality as immanent in
impulse. He assumes it to be defined by the spontaneous
gushing forth of warm feelings, warm ultimately out of concern for the private ego of the bearer.

To do one's moral duty, the old classical and Judaeo-
Christian tradition teaches, is frequently a painful, laborious
task. It requires repeated interference with our spontaneous
inclinations. Rousseau takes a sharply different view. He

28 Rousseau, *Emile*, Bk. IV, 197n.

speaks of "the pleasure of fulfilling one's duty."[29] In *Emile* he lets the Savoyard priest glorify the enjoyment of yielding to "the temptation of well-doing." "This temptation is so natural, so pleasant, that it is impossible always to resist it; and the thought of the pleasure it has once afforded is enough to recall it constantly to our memory." According to the priest, "there is nothing sweeter than virtue." How much real ethical insight is contained in these effusive admonitions to "follow the inclinations of our heart?"[30] They lack an awareness of the division in man between a higher and a lower and a recognition that the ethical course of action is often anything but easy and pleasant. Rousseau's notion of the effortlessness and pleasure of moral behavior may be contrasted against that of Aristotle, who argues that to do good man must often do what is painful. "It is on account of the pleasure that we do bad things, and on account of the pain that we abstain from noble ones."[31] When one considers that Rousseau identifies morality with particular human impulses, it is not difficult to understand his despairing of a happiness which lasts. "I doubt if it is known," he writes towards the end of his life.[32] Aristotle's teaching, by contrast, is directed precisely towards securing a happiness which endures. Ironically, Rousseau's belief in the intrinsic goodness of human nature does not give him the deeper sense of harmony described by philosophers less flattering of man.

Just as Rousseau will not hear of an unavoidable division in the human soul which makes morality frequently dependent on a difficult effort of will, he will not hear of any correspond-

29 Jean-Jacques Rousseau, *The Reveries of a Solitary*, trans. John Gould Fletcher (New York: Lennox Hill, 1971), Bk. VI, 124.
30 Rousseau, *Emile*, Bk. IV, 255.
31 Aristotle, *The Nicomachean Ethics*, trans. David Ross (London: Oxford University Press, 1954), 32 (1104b).
32 Rousseau, *Reveries*, Bk. V, 112.

ing ineradicable tension in society which threatens political unity. "Everything that destroys social unity is worthless," he writes, "and all institutions that set man at odds with himself are worthless." [33] In this statement, which is primarily directed against historical Christianity, he is in revolt against the old insight that to be at odds with oneself is the very essence of the human predicament. The classical and Judaeo-Christian tradition, too, aims for unity and harmony in the individual and society. It insists, however, that what limited progress is possible towards that goal requires continuous moral self-discipline by the individual and the support of a strong cultural tradition.

The Unity of the State

While Rousseau's egalitarian individualism leads to the endorsement of universal suffrage, it does not involve a recognition of the uniqueness of the person and of that uniqueness as an argument for limiting state control of the citizens. Universal suffrage is for Rousseau primarily a means of assuring maximum cohesion in the body politic. He is not concerned with giving the individual considerable freedom to decide his own role in society. That role is to be defined by the will of the sovereign, from which the individual is to receive "his life and his being." [34] The citizens should be "early accustomed to regard their individuality only in its relation to the body of the State, and to be aware, so to speak, of their own existence merely as a part of that of the State." [35]

In order for the general will to assert itself, Rousseau argues, "there should be no sectional associations in the

33 Rousseau, *Social Contract*, Bk. IV, Chap. VIII, 181.
34 *Ibid.*, Bk. II, Chap. VII, 84.
35 Rousseau, *Political Economy*, 307.

state."³⁶ What he disapproves of is what Robert Nisbet calls
"autonomous groups," that is, private associations between
the individual and the state with some real autonomy protected in law.³⁷ Such associations, Rousseau believes, only
divert the citizen's attachment from the state and thus diminish its authority, a view which may be compared to that of
Edmund Burke that the source of affections for the state is
our love for the private groups to which we belong.³⁸

The social pact gives to the state an "absolute power" over
its members. As though fearful of the reactions that this un-
compromising stand might elicit from his contemporaries,
Rousseau inconsistently gives his assurances that limitations
on the power of the state are built into the general will itself.
The individual needs to give up to the state only so much of
his power, goods, and liberty which is "the concern of the
community." He immediately adds, however, that "the sovereign alone is judge of what is of such concern,"³⁹ which, in
the absence of constitutional restraints, is leaving the definition to the majority of the moment.

Constitutionally protected freedoms or rights can be regarded as among other things a practical guarantee against
the state's violating the higher mission which belongs to each
individual and which can be determined in the end only by
the individual, since as a uniquely endowed person he alone
can know to what kind of life he is called by ethical conscience. Whereas in Rousseau's thought the individual person derives his entire existence from the will of the political
sovereign, the former view implies that the role of each

36 Rousseau, *Social Contract*, Bk. II, Chap. III, 73.
37 See Robert Nisbet, *Community and Power* (New York: Oxford University Press, 1962).
38 Edmund Burke, *Reflections on the Revolution in France* (London: Everyman's Library, 1964), 193.
39 Rousseau, *Social Contract*, Bk. II, Chap. IV, 74.

human being is ultimately defined with reference to a standard transcendent of all political authority. The state can be considered truly legitimate only to the extent that it respects and promotes the ability of the citizens to realize the goal known in ethical conscience. Since the latter pulls men in the direction of a common center, this view is not an invitation to anarchy. But it does place the state under a higher authority by which it can be judged and, as it were, humbled. This notion is contrary to Rousseau's political thought. Always anxious to preserve the absolute authority of the state, he rejects what he takes to be the Christianity of the Gospel: "Far from attaching the hearts of the citizens to the state, this religion detaches them from it as from all other things of this world; and I know of nothing more contrary to the social spirit." The type of "religion" he endorses derives its dogmas from the political sovereign, and these must "contain nothing contrary to the duties of the citizens."[40]

Rousseau is not satisfied with the idea that the state should have some considerable share in ordering the life of the individual and that the individual himself may regard this sharing of authority with the state as an important and necessary means towards achieving the good life. Rousseau will admit no division of authority and particularly not any constitutional recognition of such a division. He understands that if the people is to have unlimited power, nothing is more dangerous than the idea of a transcendent moral standard. If men's ultimate allegiance is to an ethical conscience beyond and above all political authority, there is no longer any hope for undivided loyalty to the state. It means, as Lester Crocker puts it, that "the individual conscience might at times be morally superior to the law, or at least consider itself as such.

40 *Ibid.*, Bk. IV, Chap. VIII, 182, 187.

And then we could bid adieu to the collective, organic unity of the political body." [41]

Nationalism and Military Virtue

We have noted that in the unity of the public person Rousseau wants to re-create man's natural freedom. But why is that cohesion so important? What is the content of the freedom of the general will? One sign that the true will of the sovereign is actually being expressed, Rousseau argues, is that "public opinion approaches unanimity." [42] Conversely, prolonged debate and dissension is a sign that selfish interests are uppermost in the minds of the citizens. Using these criteria, one wonders how one should view a Nazi mass meeting where the proposals regarding the destiny of the German people advanced by the Führer—who might conceivably be considered a modern counterpart of the lawgiver or the temporary dictator, or some combination of the two—are greeted with the spontaneous and enthusiastic approval of a unified assembly. Whatever the merit of this particular illustration, there are numerous indications in *The Social Contract* and elsewhere that Rousseau's emphasis on political unity is at least partly based on an association of the general will with nationalism and even militarism. "Do we wish men to be virtuous," he asks. "Then let us begin by making them love their country." [43]

It is interesting to note that in spite of all arguments designed to establish the absolute authority of the general will, Rousseau never presents it as supra-national. On the con-

41 Lester G. Crocker, *Rousseau's Social Contract: An Interpretive Essay* (Cleveland: Press of Case Western Reserve University, 1968), 11.
42 Rousseau, *Social Contract*, Bk. IV, Chap. II, 151.
43 Rousseau, *Political Economy*, 302.

trary, although he toys with the idea of a federation of states, he views the general will in the international arena as a sectional, particularistic will, something he dreads in the individual state. "The will of the State, though general in relation to its own members, is no longer so in relation to other States and their members, but becomes, for them, a particular and individual will, which has its rule of justice in the law of nature."[44] What concerns us here about this statement is not the clear contradiction of the interpretation that the general will is a universal, transcendent moral standard, but the way in which Rousseau transfers the freedom of the natural man to the various public persons in the world. These acquire the natural freedom that the individual person has lost forever. It should be carefully noted, however, that in this new state of nature enjoyed by whole states conditions come much closer to Hobbes's conception than to Rousseau's in the *Discourses*. The general wills of the states are likely to clash. Even among states based on the social contract "the weak are always in danger of being swallowed up" by the strong. The reason is that "all peoples generate a kind of centrifugal force, by which they brush continuously against one another, and they all attempt to expand at the expense of their neighbours."[45] The general will, one is forced to conclude, has in it an element of nationalistic expansionism. It is necessary to go further and say that it also has a militaristic coloring. *The Social Contract* contains numerous approving references to Spartan, military virtues. One of Rousseau's main complaints against traditional Christianity is that it makes the citizens poor soldiers. The militaristic tendency is prominent also in other works, such as the *First Discourse* and *The Government of Poland*. It is closely associated with a preference for

44 *Ibid.*, 290.
45 Rousseau, *Social Contract*, Bk. II, Chap. IX, 92. See also Chaps. IX–X, *passim*.

nationalism. "It is certain," Rousseau writes, "that the greatest miracles of virtue have been produced by patriotism."[46]

The nationalistic and militaristic bias in Rousseau's political thought is reflected in several of his statements regarding the goal of the state. In *The Social Contract* he points out, for example, that "the only way in which [men] can preserve themselves is by uniting their separate powers in a combination strong enough to overcome any resistance."[47] In several places he states as the goal of the state the self-preservation and protection of the members.[48] He offers in the latter part of *Emile* two standards for the "goodness" of the state. One is an increase in population. The other is the distribution of population. About the latter he writes that two states of equal size and population may still be very unequal in strength. "The more powerful is always that in which the people are more evenly distributed over its territory." The goodness of the state is here judged primarily by military criteria.[49]

Although Rousseau also speaks of "*freedom* and *equality*" as the goal of the state,[50] his numerous expressions of nationalistic and militaristic sentiments would seem to indicate that equality is primarily a domestic objective of the individual state. The possibility is clearly left open that internationally the freedom of the public person may entail liberty for the powerful states to expand imperialistically at the expense of the weaker. Again, the alleged morality of the general will is placed in a curious light.

Unless one penetrates to the very heart of Rousseau's

46 Rousseau, *Political Economy*, 301.
47 Rousseau, *Social Contract*, Bk. I, Chap. VI, 59–60.
48 See, for example, Rousseau, *Social Contract*, Bk. I, Chap. VI; Bk. III, Chap. IX, 130; Bk. IV, Chap. I, 149; Bk. IV, Chap. VI, 171; Bk. IV, Chap. VIII, *passim*.
49 Rousseau, *Emile*, Bk. IV, 432–33. *Cf.* Rousseau, *Social Contract*, Bk. II, Chap. X, 93 and Bk. III, Chap. IX, 130.
50 Rousseau, *Social Contract*, Bk. II, Chap. XI, 96.

moral theory and can interpret it with reference to its central motive, there will seem to be an irreconcilable conflict between military and social discipline, on the one hand, and liberation of man's spontaneity, on the other. The conflict disappears when it is understood that Rousseau is attributing social cohesiveness and various other desirable characteristics to the spontaneous selves of the citizens. Individuals all acting from inside their true nature spontaneously form a unified, public-spirited community. In the good state, social harmony does not require an effort of individual self-discipline as that term is used in the classical and Judaeo-Christian traditions. It is supplied by the natural inclinations of the citizens. Rousseau's view that the general will may have to force some citizens to be free should be interpreted accordingly. The force in question will seem an external intrusion only to those who are not yet acting in the spirit of their original nature but are caught in the oppressive patterns of traditional civilization. The force would be employed by those already acting from inside their true selves and with the purpose of liberating the goodness of their less fortunate fellows. We may understand Rousseau to mean that whatever restraining activity and propaganda are necessary in the new state are needed only because men will continue to be influenced, at least for some time, by the alien, perverting patterns of behavior inherited from the old society. They must be guided to discovery of their true nature.

In his proclivity for nationalism and militarism, which culminates in the work on the government of Poland, Rousseau appears to be ascribing to the general will a content difficult to reconcile with certain other descriptions of the same will. Whether these sentiments are to be regarded as only an aberration or as an integral part of his philosophy is probably the wrong question to ask, for at the root of his thinking is not so much a belief in some enduring principle of life as a passion for unrestrained freedom, a freedom associated moreover with his own predilections and preferences. We may venture the interpretation that Rousseau's conception of the general will is deeply colored, if not completely determined, by his own temperament, which is allowed to roam freely. His nationalistic and militaristic inclinations may be viewed as one example of his reading into the general will what his own "heart" happens to be craving. In certain writings, like *Emile*, where he is primarly concerned with an ideal for private life, the tendency is anarchistic; in writings like *The Social Contract*, where he is dealing with collective, political life, his preference for unlimited freedom takes on a Spartan quality. In the latter work he brings together a pervasive hostility to restraint with a wish for discipline, such as might be found in an unruly rebel who is called to repentance by his own conscience. Rousseau envisions the subordination of the individual to a higher authority. He does so in all too characteristic fashion, however, without putting man under the painful obligation of actually making a moral effort. Men shall achieve virtue by participating in the general will of the people, which is nothing but their own spontaneous will. Although the release of that first impulse in all men may necessitate some constraining interference with others by those already liberated, morality itself requires of the individual only that he listen to his heart and yield effortlessly to its pleasant command.

Utopian Dreams and Harsh Realities

It has not been my purpose to deny that Rousseau's concept of the general will has features which connect it with the real, transcendent standard of morality of which most men have some awareness. I have only tried to show that in its central inspiration this concept owes more to Rousseau's utopian-romantic imagination. What is genuine ethical insight in his thought, for such there is too, is subordinated to and vitiated by the spurious, subjectively inspired tendency of his philosophy as a whole. To a degree, subjective bias enters into all intellectual undertakings. The point is that, although offered under the pretentions of objective philosophical inquiry, Rousseau's thought has in it too much of that element to provide a strong link between moral philosophy and democratic theory.

It is difficult to dispel the suspicion that in large part the general will is a projection of Rousseau's unfailing belief in the superior goodness of his own heart onto the people. He views the will of the sovereign in the light of what he perceives to be his own divinely inspired spontaneity. During his life Rousseau became ever more convinced of his own moral innocence and the vice and deceit of other men. He regarded himself as always inclined towards the good and thwarted only by various outer restraints from achieving his worthy goals. "Never has the moral instinct deceived me," he writes. Late in his life he talks of giving back to his Author "a host of good but frustrated intentions." [1] It is not surprising that Rousseau would like to see released in political society the collective counterpart of the spontaneous goodness which he believes to have been denied expression in his personal life. That he likes to substitute for the imperfect world around him the more appealing creations of his own imagination, he freely admits. Into nature especially, where he does not have to contend with the depravity and conceit of society, he finds it easy to project his dreams and emotions. His worship of nature, it may be argued, is in no small part worship of his own elevated sentiments. What is it, he asks in a revealing passage, which always brings him back to the "inanimate objects" of nature? "What secret charm brings me back constantly into your midst? Unfeeling and dead things, this charm is not in you; it could not be there. It is in my own heart which wishes to refer back everything to itself." [2] This, let it be suggested, is the central inspiration also of the concept of the general will. Rousseau is reading into it the imagined morality of his own largely subjective and historically conditioned preferences regarding the organization and goal of the state. He is assuming that he has full knowledge of man's true nature and that the heart of all men craves the same political arrangements as does his own.

It should be remembered in this context that Rousseau does not start from, but emphatically rejects, the notion of man as a social being. To him, civil society is, in the literal meaning of the word, *artificial*. The sociopolitical nature of

1 Jean-Jacques Rousseau, *The Reveries of a Solitary*, trans. John Gould Fletcher (New York: Lennox Hill, 1971), Bk. IV, 85; Bk. II, 46.
2 Quoted in P. M. Masson, *La Religion de J.-J. Rousseau* (3 Vols.; Paris: Lennox Hill, 1916), II, 228. Translated in Irving Babbitt, *Rousseau and Romanticism* (Cleveland: World Publishing Co., Meridian Books, 1964), 233.

man has to be created. As he writes in *The Social Contract*,
"The constitution of a man is the work of nature; that of the
state is the work of artifice [*de l'art*]." [3] We may regard Rousseau as himself the ultimate artist, the philosopher with the
remedy for all the ills of existing society. His general will is a
product of his "creative imagination" rather than an acceptable conceptual rendering of the real principle of morality. Regardless of the extent to which Rousseau's temperament
influences his thinking, it is evident that the general will is
not to be mistaken for the transcendent will of ethical conscience. His concept arbitrarily elevates a particularistic, national will, moral only by allegation and with strong totalitarian implications, to a position of absolute authority. The
common good of political society is for Rousseau not the imperfect representation of a standard transcendent of politics,
but the immanent manifestation of perfect morality in the
will of the people.

Superficially, Rousseau's thinking in *The Social Contract* is
an endorsement of democracy and the people's right to self-
government. It should be clear, however, that the people is
also an instrument for Rousseau's subjective imagination. If
his assumptions regarding the spontaneous direction of the
popular will have little to sustain them in real life, his democratic formulas are meaningless abstractions, asking to be
used by those who want to exercise power dictatorially in the
name of the people. If Rousseau's conception of the general
will grows out of an essentially utopian view of human nature, he is also offering an essentially utopian view of how
democracy can be made to respect and promote the ethical
life. *The Social Contract* has very doubtful value as a theory of
democracy and a source of inspiration for political action, for

---

3 Jean-Jacques Rousseau, *The Social Contract*, trans. Maurice Cranston (Harmondsworth: Penguin Books, 1968), Bk. III, Chap. XI, 135.

unlike Plato's *Republic*, for instance, its utopianism does not have the saving grace of being grounded in an adequate definition of the fundamental problem of morality. Plato may be criticized for exaggerating man's ability to solve that problem, but hardly for evading it. Rousseau's philosophy, on the other hand, simply assumes the goodness of human nature and ignores the need for moral self-discipline in the individual and the people. For that reason he may be accused of preparing the way, not for a morally inspired democratic order, but for political partisanship and arbitrariness. No amount of utopian assurances about the goodness of the spontaneous will of the people can remove the only too real and persistent lower inclinations of human nature as we know it in history.

The idea that man's first impulse is good and will show itself as such on a large scale under the proper political circumstances is theoretical in a very questionable sense. It can be maintained only in the teeth of normal experience. Rousseau himself admits that to realize the goals of *The Social Contract* a new man will be needed, one bearing little resemblance to the creature of vice and artificiality found in actual societies. Yet, Rousseau offers no real proof that his psychological premises are anything more than hopes and dreams. Insofar as Rousseau's personal life is any indication of what kind of man will emerge when hostility to restraint and conventional social responsibility is adopted as a principle of conduct, one is forced to face the rather striking contrast between the utopian-romantic ideal and the real.[4]

Experience suggests that man's first impulse is far from always good. Indeed, it would seem to be more in keeping with the facts to say that it tends in the opposite direction,

---

4 *Cf.* Babbitt, *Rousseau and Romanticism*, especially Chaps. 4–5.

towards some kind of selfishness or arbitrariness. Men acquire some moral virtue and steadiness precisely to the extent that they become accustomed to *arresting* the impulse of the moment and subjecting it to moral scrutiny before acting. The ethical life, I have argued, needs the support of sound tradition and custom. These help to build into human action a pattern of habit by which impulse is restrained and organized with reference to a higher standard. The purpose of civilization is to liberate man's higher potential by disciplining his spontaneity, which by itself tends away from all order. In Rousseau's view, however, civilization has been an instrument of enslavement: "Our wisdom is slavish prejudice, our customs consist in control, constraint, compulsion. Civilised man is born and dies a slave." [5] Where there should be complete freedom for man's natural inclinations there are inhibiting and perverting cultural norms. Whatever "civilization" will be needed in the true state is apparently expected by Rousseau to flow out of man as a sort of by-product of morality once the latter has been released in society. Granted that there must be morally questionable elements in any tradition, Rousseau's blanket denunciation of existing civilization is, practically speaking, a denial of the need for the formative guidance of culture in the ethical life.

Viewed realistically, one effect of applying Rousseau's teaching to life would be to relax or remove the fetters which restrain man's lower nature. And, as Burke points out, the less control exercised by the individual internally, the more will have to be imposed from without by the state. Lack of moral self-discipline on the part of a people invites anarchy and increases the danger of political dictatorship. To the extent that Rousseau's recommendations were followed, the

5 Jean-Jacques Rousseau, *Emile*, trans. Barbara Foxley (London: Everyman's Library, 1969), Bk. I, 10.

general will, which needs to respect no higher moral or constitutional authority, would in all likelihood turn out in practice to be a highly arbitrary expression of majority opinion. Political cohesion would probably have to be supplied in the end by some disciplined organization, centrally led and claiming to act for the common good of the people. In international affairs, one might expect "the will of the people" to exhibit the same lack of restraint. Very possibly, it would turn out to be nationalistic and expansionistic.

Rousseau's ideas have had an enormous influence. The notion that morality is the result of yielding to the goodness of our first impulse is bound to appeal to man's all too natural inclination to escape the effort and pain of actual moral self-improvement. Placing the blame for all social ills not really on man himself but on his environment has also won Rousseau many followers. His political thought is more flattering than realistic. Unfortunately, his influence as a theorist of democracy is partially due to the fact that he ignores certain unpleasant truths, which reduce considerably the optimism with which popular rule may be contemplated. The achievement of the common good, he thinks, is not dependent on a difficult process of moral self-reform, involving protracted cultural assimilation, by which the citizens develop a measure of political responsibility. It does not require that this responsibility be promoted and protected by constitutional laws, written or unwritten. On the contrary, the good of society is best served by *removing* all restraints on the momentary will of popular majorities. This belief, we may say in conclusion, is in essence a utopian dream sustained by large doses of moral conceit. It is evident that an adequate theory of the reconciliation of democracy with the ethical life must rest on a more realistic assessment of human nature and politics.

PART FOUR

The Ethics of
Constitutional Democracy

Constitutionalism and Popular Sovereignty

So far we have sought mostly by elimination to determine how popular self-government can be made compatible with the needs of the ethical life. I have tried to show that Rousseau's influential theory of democracy does not come to grips with man's moral predicament. Only because he denies that man's baser inclinations are a part of the essence of human nature and assumes the morality of the spontaneous popular will can he advance his notion of plebiscitary rule, according to which the majority of the moment is allowed to set public policy. If it is true as I have argued that man is not spontaneously propelled in the direction of morality, democratic theory must instead concern itself with the need for ethical self-discipline and look for the political means by which such discipline can be promoted. I have intimated that some form of constitutionalism is called for.

The American Constitution

Constitutional democracy we define broadly as popular rule under legal restraints which cannot be changed or removed without the support of a qualified majority over an extended period of time. Our analysis of this concept may be brought into closer contact with the institutional problems of democracy by using the American constitution as an illustration. In so doing I am not suggesting that its particular provisions are necessarily the best available example of this type of democracy, only that they offer a good practical illustration of the general principle.

One of the rules generally regarded as essential to the definition of democracy is that with some possible exceptions all adults should have the right to affect government policy through voting and be eligible for public office. The authors of the United States Constitution did not envision "universal suffrage" in the modern sense of the word. They left the qualifications for the right to vote up to the individual states, assuming only that popular participation would be comparatively widespread, as was already the case at the time. Perceived from the beginning as more democratic than the governments of the leading European countries and soon viewed by foreign observers like Alexis de Tocqueville as the very embodiment of popular rule, the American constitutional system has only had its democratic reputation enhanced by the extension of popular suffrage. Although this development was not prescribed in the original document, one is justified in thinking of the system of government it regulates as democratic with regard to popular participation.

Does it follow that we must accept Abraham Lincoln's description of American government as government for the people, by the people, and of the people? Curiously, from the point of view of much modern democratic theory, this allegedly democratic form of government is not designed to maximize the influence of popular majorities. Indeed, the founding fathers had no wish to create a "democracy," claiming instead that the Constitution established a "republic." One might even say that through its system of checks and balances it tends to thwart the will of the momentary national majority. In fact, the people, viewed as an undifferentiated mass, is not even given constitutional recognition. There is no institutional channel through which a mere numerical majority can work its will. The "people" of the constitution is made up of a number of overlapping, subdivided electorates. Not even the president is chosen by a national majority. He is selected by a majority of the Electoral College, a body chosen by pluralities in the various states and according to a formula which further ignores the national majority by giving over-representation, by numerical standards, to the smaller states. The members of the Senate and House are elected by pluralities of yet other electorates (the Senate originally by the state legislatures). To the extent that the undifferentiated mass of the people or a majority thereof can be said to have a unified political will at all, there is no point in the American system of government where that will can be applied. The electoral processes of American democracy are far removed from what might perhaps be regarded as the plebiscitary ideal, the national referendum on public policy.

The same anti-plebiscitary slant marks the process whereby policy is made by the federal government. The Constitution prescribes a division of power between an executive, legislative, and judicial branch. In order for a bill to get passed it must not only be approved by both houses of Congress, which are made up of members beholden to different electorates in their home states, but signed by the president. The chief executive in turn is required to get the approval of the Senate for certain important acts, such as the appointment of high-level officials in the executive branch. In its implied power of "judicial review," that is, of passing on the constitutionality of acts of the other branches of government, the Supreme Court is a check on each. The justices of the Supreme Court are appointed by the president with the approval of the Senate. They could be removed by the Senate only under unusual circumstances, and then after a vote of impeachment in the House of Representatives, a congressional power of last resort hanging also over the head of the president. Another important feature of the elaborate system of checks and balances, of which I am only giving a very general and incomplete account, is the division of power between federal and state government, the Constitution designating the proper role of each. In the central area of constitutional amendment, the method that has actually been used (out of two available procedures) requires concurrence between a large majority of the states and Congress.

Since no merely temporary majority of the people, however large, can acquire control over all the levels and branches of government, its power is severely limited. It is possible to imagine a presidential election year in which popular passions run so strongly in a definite direction that the result is not only the election of a president favorable to the cause, but a staggering and equally favorable majority in the House of Representatives and among those winning the third of the Senate seats to be filled that year. Even that is not enough to assure the full public implementation of the popular demand in question. The senators who make up the two thirds of the Senate previously elected will not necessarily concur in the sentiments now sweeping the country. And their independence is protected by the Constitution, as is that of any popular representative at the federal level—be it a senator, a member of the House, or a president. Provided that a majority of the Senate, or even a very powerful two thirds of that body, does not acquiesce, the attempt to implement the popular will of the moment has been thwarted. And even if the necessary votes are available in the Senate, the Constitution itself is still in effect, prescribing the procedures by which government policy has to be determined and at the same time limiting its scope.

The idea of representation associated with American government deserves special attention. According to "Publius" in *The Federalist Papers*, the representative institutions provided for in the Constitution are not intended to be mere reflectors of public opinion. They are supposed to contribute to the "refinement" of the will of the people. According to Federalist Paper number 10 (Madison), the delegation of authority to representative institutions is designed to "refine and enlarge the public views by passing them through the medium of a chosen body of citizens, whose wisdom may best discern the true interest of their country and whose patriotism and love of justice will be least likely to sacrifice it to temporary or partial considerations." [1]

It should be noted that by giving many of the popular representatives very substantial terms of office—as long as six years for senators and four years for presidents—the Constitution relieves them to a considerable degree from popular pressure. Their staying in office is not dependent on being always in tune with public opinion. They have the opportunity to follow their own best judgment even when it might be in sharp conflict with the wishes expressed by the people. They can do so in the hope that by the time their electors are to pass on their performance at the polls, their stand will have been vindicated or their integrity will have earned them the respect of erstwhile opponents. The same freedom to deviate from or even defy the public opinion of the moment is available to members of the House of Representatives, although their inclinations to exercise independent judgment

1 Hamilton, Madison, and Jay, *The Federalist Papers*, ed. Clinton Rossiter (New York: Mentor Books, 1961), No. 10, p. 82.

may not be quite as strong, since their relatively short term of office does not offer the same protection against popular dissatisfaction and electoral censure. On the whole, the nature and role of representative institutions in the United States tend to make elections not so much referenda on specific policies as opportunities to elect individuals believed to have the qualifications to make decisions on their own in their constituents' behalf.

In the case of the Supreme Court, popular control is at a minimum. The voting public affects the composition of the Court only by electing the president and the Senate, in the first instance indirectly, in the second instance directly (since 1913). These together appoint the justices. Once on the Court, moreover, a justice cannot be removed, except under extreme conditions. Obviously, this gives him a marked independence in relation to public opinion, if he chooses to exercise it.

The American form of government can be said to place ultimate political authority in the hands of the people. But the people is not given, or does not give itself, the power to do what it pleases in the short run. The current majority is always subject to the restraints of checks and balances. Only a majority which is, or becomes, both persistent and overwhelming can work its will completely, to the point of removing constitutional obstacles which stand in the way of the full realization of its wishes. The net effect of these legal restraints is to put on the momentary majority the burden of proof. In order to acquire decisive power it must become more than a momentary and merely partisan majority. It must prove itself over time as having a will worthy of broad support. In the words of Willmoore Kendall: "The American political system is not and never has been a system for the automatic acceptance of majority mandates by the minority. It is not and never has been a system for the large-scale coercion of the minority. . . . Under the American political system *the majority bides its time until it can act by consensus.*" [2]

The Idea of Popular Sovereignty

But is not this to make a mockery of the democratic ideal? Must not a true democracy always promote the maximum of popular control over public policy? Does not popular suffrage in the American form of government just barely conceal the authoritarian nature of the system as a whole? Surely, this elaborate thwarting of the will of the majority is incompatible with the idea of popular sovereignty. The objection brings us to the heart of the fundamental issue which has to be decided by democratic theory. Granted that popular sovereignty must be basic to democracy, what are we to understand by it?

It would seem that when we attribute to the people the right of self-government, we can mean one of two things. One is that the people should be free at every turn to act as it pleases. The other is that the people may act only under certain restraints. To say that only the first meaning is compatible with the idea of popular sovereignty is to fall either into self-contradiction or utopian thinking. If the idea means complete freedom for the people to act, it does not rule out the abolition of democracy and the establishment of dictatorship. That would turn popular sovereignty into a useless concept. The proposition that the people may do as it pleases cannot be saved by saying that of course the people must not give up the democratic form of government, for that is to adopt the second proposition, namely that popular sov-

---

2 Willmore Kendall, *Contra Mundum*, ed. Nellie D. Kendall (New Rochelle, N.Y.: Arlington House, 1971), 277–78 (emphasis in original).

ereignty involves limiting the people's freedom. The only way to defend it would be to take a Rousseauistic approach, attempting to prove that under certain circumstances it will always please the people to act so that popular control is perpetuated. But as we have seen, not even Rousseau is unequivocal in his assertion of the ascendancy of the general will over the tyrannical will of all in his ideal state. Unless we are to make certain blatantly unrealistic assumptions about the necessary and powerful presence of democratic preferences in the people, we are left with the proposition that limitations on the popular will are not only compatible with but actually implied in the notion of popular sovereignty. What we might regard as the general principle of constitutionalism would thus seem to be inseparable from the concept itself. The question becomes: by whom are these limitations to be determined in scope and by whom applied? In a democracy, presumably, the answer must be, by the people or its representatives.

Paradoxically, insofar as popular rule is a real concept and not just some utopian dream, it refers to government by the people under self-imposed restraints. The meaning of the latter idea must be carefully analyzed. Since it is our purpose to investigate the compatibility of democracy with the needs of the ethical life, we shall be primarily interested in exploring its ethical dimension.

Rousseau's ideal is a people of one political will. He can entertain it because he is assuming the essential unity of human nature. If we do not have recourse to his type of imagination, however, but base our thinking on what can be observed in actual societies, we are forced to recognize the existence of a chronic conflict of wills, in large matters and small. Widespread agreement between the citizens is sometimes achieved and maintained in certain areas, but the unlikelihood of

popular unanimity in politics explains the prominence in
democratic theory of the concepts of majority and minority.
Just as there are different political wills at work in a people at
any particular time, there are different wills at work over a
span of time. Public opinion presents an ever-changing con-
stellation of views and sentiments. There are continuous
shifts of emphasis and variations in intensity. The lines of
confrontation are repeatedly redrawn. Majorities are transformed into minorities, minorities transformed into majorities. To what in this varied stream of popular opinion is
sovereignty to be attached? We have already seen that it
does not belong to just any expression of will. An answer may
be suggested by drawing on the ethical philosophy I have advanced.

I have argued that man is a creature of two worlds. His life
is a tension between a perpetual and always changing flow of
impulses and a sense of higher purpose. Whenever affirmed
by man, this higher will disciplines and structures his wishes
of the moment with a view to the enduring moral good. It
builds into his life a measure of unity and harmony, a certain
approximation of human imperfection to transcendent perfection. Except in the sense that ethical conscience reveals
itself to every person in unique circumstances, it is not some
private guide to what is good. It wills the universal end for
man, unifying the multiplicity of human acts in itself. I have
referred to this self-justifying goal as "harmony," "happiness,"
and "community," using words which describe aspects of
the same reality. The ultimate end of politics may be defined
as community. By this word I mean a special type of association, a civilized living together in which the intellectual,
aesthetic, and economic life of society serves the moral destiny shared by all. In religious terminology, this destiny is
ultimately community with God. Referring to the partial

realization of this goal which lies within the reach of politics and which is of concern to us here, Aristotle speaks of "the good life."

Just as an individual is always under an obligation to act morally in his "private" affairs, so is he under an obligation to act morally when he is performing "public" or "political" acts, such as casting a vote in an election. The term *people* used in democratic theory does not signify some mysterious, independent entity hovering over the heads of the individual citizens. It is the collective name for those same individuals acting in their capacity as political participants. Ethical conscience wills the same goal in all men, the widest possible sharing in community. Just as each person has a higher self, therefore, the whole people, made up as it is of individual citizens, also has a higher self, namely ethical conscience as it relates to "public" or "political" matters. As the common self of the citizens organized for the purpose of conducting their common affairs, it seeks, not the partisan advantage of any person or group, but the kind of political order which is conducive to the spiritual elevation of society. Against this higher will, in need of no special pleading, stands an infinite number of possible factional popular wishes which detract from the moral goal and can be defined in contradistinction as the people's lower will.

A people can thus be said to have two selves, one which always wills the same, the promotion of community in given circumstances, and one with an always varying content tending to divert the political order to merely partisan objectives. But then we must ask this question about the idea of popular self-rule: what self is to rule? The only morally defensible answer is that it must be the *higher* self of the people, or, if that phrase has too much of a metaphysical ring, the will to community in the individual citizens. Since in my analysis of

Rousseau and in other places I have emphatically rejected the idea of identity between morality and politics, I am obviously not suggesting that democracy becomes acceptable only if the people can be expected to decide everything in accordance with ethical conscience. What I am contending is that the concept of democracy is ethically defensible only if it conceives of popular self-rule as designed in such a way as to *promote* the application of ethical conscience to political issues. Whatever other types of self-imposed limitations are implied in the idea of popular sovereignty, the people has to impose some moral discipline on itself. In other words, popular sovereignty must be defined with reference to the ethical standard of community.

But is there not something undemocratic about this notion that the people must subject itself to a superior in the form of an ethical purpose? Granted that the majority must not suddenly decide to abolish the democratic rules of the game, is not that view in reality hostile to the whole idea of popular self-government and freedom? That would be true only if one would also have to say that a person is not governing himself, but resigning his freedom, who is seeking to guide his behavior by ethical conscience. But this discipline is self-imposed. It is the willing affirmation of good. The structuring role of ethical conscience is not viewed by the individual as some alien, external interference with his life but as something necessary to the fulfillment of his own humanity. To call it a curtailment of freedom is to transform the idea of freedom into a formula for unhappiness.

Freedom can be adequately understood only in conjunction with the moral worth of chosen goals, so that a person is free in the most profound philosophical sense only to the extent that by his actions he enriches and fulfills his life. Community being the highest value, happiness lies in the widest possible sharing of the good life with others. Freedom, therefore, is properly the ability to act with concern for what promotes the spiritual well-being of all affected. In the strictest sense, a people can be said to be exercising freedom in governing itself only when it is genuinely trying to realize the conditions of community.

The democratic "freedoms"—freedom of expression, of association, etc.—are appropriately labeled such, for in a world of finite insight and endless change and diversity, they give recognition to the need for constant examination and reexamination of means and to the need for protection of the uniqueness of mission belonging to each individual by virtue of his special gifts and circumstances in life. Political freedoms are not ends in themselves. When their exercise is detached from a concern for the common good, they degenerate into opportunities for private aggrandizement and license. They become an endorsement of the politically and morally destructive forces of society. Popular majorities feeding on that type of "freedom" are in effect conspiratorial groups seeking to expand at the expense of competitors. To define popular sovereignty as attaching to this kind of popular will is to base the definition of democracy on what is inherently destructive of the very existence of this and other forms of government.

The Spirit
of Constitutionalism

X

Insofar as it is compatible with the needs of the ethical life, democracy seeks to promote a certain quality of popular will. This leads us to the role of the constitution. It may be viewed in analogy with the rules or principles which the individual person adopts for his "private" behavior. Aware of his own moral and other weaknesses, he gives sovereignty not to his impulse of the moment but to standards of conduct which he has pledged not to change or abrogate on whim or under the pressure of passion, but only after careful and sober deliberation. A constitution serves a similar function in the public realm. It is a standard of political behavior which is not supposed to be changed on the spur of the moment, but only through an elaborate procedure which enhances the likelihood that the decision be made when the emotions are calm and respectable motives uppermost. Needless to say, only people of high moral culture will subject their political wishes to constitutional restraints for the specific purpose of advancing the goal of community. Where citizens are lacking in this respect they will accept restraints, if at all, only as a way of advancing their own personal advantage. They may endorse the constitutional objective of leaving an appeal from the people drunk to the people sober, but that would be a means of promoting enlightened self-interest as distinguished from narrow-minded, short-sighted self-interest. There is a certain similarity between constitutionalism inspired by moral motives and constitutionalism inspired by mere sophisticated egotism. Both have the effect of curbing the expansiveness of the lower will of individuals and groups. I have argued previously that men's ability to discern what is in their own enlightened self-interest depends in the end on their having some notion, however vague, of what transcends the calculus of private advantage. [1]

But in order to establish the moral necessity of constitutionalism we need to state with more precision its relation to ethical conscience. A constitution, it may be said in general, is a recognition of the need to put checks on the tendency of individuals and groups to impose their own idea of what is politically desirable on others. It is an attempt to purge politics of blatant arbitrariness. Specific designations of power and various procedural requirements, whether prescribed by long-honored precedence or a written document, counteract the inclination to proceed with disregard for the rest of society. The requirement to follow a fundamental law gives a measure of impartiality to the formulation and implementation of public policy. It tends to promote a detachment of government from various competing special interests. The law, not any particular will, is sovereign. Short of destruction of the political order, the strong are not free to crush the weak. The latter are left an appeal against raw power. The very opposite of arbitrariness in politics would be correspondence between the political influence of individual citizens and groups and their contribution to community. No constitution can accomplish this goal. It can only be an attempt to limit the influence of selfish interests, not by eradicating them, which is impossible, but by taming them. In a democracy that

1 See Chap. I, herein, pp. 25–26.

means that the majority of the moment is not given total freedom to dictate policy. To do so would be to maximize the
influence of the tendency, present to some degree in most expressions of political will, to disregard the good of the whole.

To become an effective regulating force a constitution
must have the support of the citizens. Since the moral capacity of a people is limited, this support must also be found in a
nonmoral source. For an elaboration of this point we may
draw on one of the most original of American thinkers, John
C. Calhoun. His constitutional reasoning is of interest here
because it recognizes the existence of a common good in the
higher sense while being adjusted to the preponderance of
self-interest as a motivating force in politics. Calhoun is re-
conciled to the fact that the latter state of affairs cannot be
drastically changed and that therefore self-interest somehow
must be turned into the service of the common good, a need
to which I have previously alluded.[2] It should be made clear
that there is no necessary relationship between those of Calhoun's arguments that will be considered here and the
specific, and to my mind rather awkward, institutional arrangements he proposes for the United States.

Concern for merely private advantage, Calhoun believes,
must be restrained by constitutional checks. The only way
that these checks can be made effective, however, is for the
provisions of the constitution to give power to, and thereby
become aligned with, various major interests which can help
to enforce them in practice. The self-interest of each portion
of the community which is recognized by the constitution can
be counted upon to restrain the self-interest of other groups.
"It is this negative power—the power of preventing or arresting the action of the government, be it called by what term it
may, veto, interposition, nullification, check, or balance of

2 See Chap. I, herein, p. 22; Chap. III, p. 86; and Chap. VI, pp. 109–11.

power—which in fact forms the constitution. . . . Without this there can be no negative, and without a negative, no constitution." [3]

The American constitution with its elaborate system of checks and balances exhibits at least the likeness of the kind of "negative" on government which Calhoun is describing. It has a general effect of great ethical interest. The Constitution makes a consideration of the needs and wishes of numerous groups a requirement for a majority that wishes to achieve any part of its program. The approximation of a consensus is needed before government policy can be made. Competing groups, whether in the majority or the minority, are induced from the very start to adopt a politically inclusive perspective. To further their own cause, that same cause must be defined with a view to making it acceptable to other groups that might otherwise veto it.

This built-in inducement to consider the wishes of other groups will not necessarily, and indeed only in exceptional cases, lead to the adoption of a genuinely moral point of view, that is, to a subordination of private advantage to the needs of the common good. But it does tend to reduce the element of blatant self-seeking and thus to give some support to the moral aspirations also present in the people and its representatives. The self-restraints suggested by mere enlightened self-interest, it should be carefully noted, do not in themselves have any moral worth. But paradoxically they greatly facilitate the task of those who are striving to give politics a higher direction. These citizens can to some extent enlist the selfishly inspired restraint of others in support of the moral end. They may even be able to transform it by an appeal to ethical conscience. Since politics is not normally, if ever, a

---

3 John C. Calhoun, *A Disquisition on Government and Selections from the Discourses*, ed. C. Gordon Post (New York: Bobbs-Merrill Co., 1953), 28.

sphere of morally elevated activity, the ethical importance of this point can hardly be exaggerated. What might perhaps be called the Hobbesian intellectual tradition goes too far when it makes egotism the sole structuring principle of politics. There is as great a need, however, to guard against conceptions of politics which are based on unrealistic or even naïve expectations about the degree to which morality can take the place of self-interest.

This reasoning ties in with Calhoun's argument in favor of government by "concurrent majority." We may cite his description of the contrast between that form of government and one of simple majority rule, by "numerical majority" in his terminology.

The same cause which in governments of the numerical majority gives to party attachments and antipathies such force as to place party triumph and ascendancy above the safety and prosperity of the community will just as certainly give them sufficient force to overpower all regard for truth, justice, sincerity, and moral obligations of every description. . . . In the government of the concurrent majority, on the contrary, the same cause which prevents such strife as the means of obtaining power, and which makes it the interest of each portion to conciliate and promote the interests of the others, would exert a powerful influence toward purifying and elevating the character of the government and the people, morally as well as politically.[4]

What is of interest to our present argument is not whether the specific institutional suggestions offered by Calhoun will accomplish the stated goal, but the principle itself: in a government of concurrent majority self-interest is checked by self-interest in such a way that, willy-nilly, it becomes a potential support for moral aspirations. The extent to which a constitution will actually promote such aspirations, however,

4 *Ibid.*, 38–39.

will depend entirely on the extent to which the perpetual conflict of interests is leavened by the motive of community among the political participants. To serve the higher goal the constitution must be sustained by considerable moral culture.

A constitution, then, is an attempt to purge politics of the kind of egotism which would crush everything in its way. Insofar as it is inspired by the moral motive, it aims even further, to the *substitution* of ethical conscience for enlightened self-interest as the ordering principle of politics. It then becomes the institutional embodiment of the rejection, not only of the kind of arbitrariness which threatens the peaceful balancing of group interests, but of every form of arbitrariness. Its provisions become a means of lifting politics in the direction of fulfillment of a higher law. As Walter Lippmann writes, "Constitutional restraints and bills of rights, the whole apparatus of responsible government and of an independent judiciary, the conception of due process of law in courts, in legislatures, among executives, are but the rough approximations by which men have sought to exorcise the devil of arbitrariness in human relations."[5] Although always imperfect and less than successful, constitutions serve their highest purpose by allowing the censuring of "caprice and willfulness" with a view to the *moral* end. Drawing on Plato, John Hallowell observes: "The absolute identification of moral and social restraints is possible only in an ideal state; and, while actual states always fall short of this ideal, the measure of their statehood is the degree to which that ideal is realized."[6]

5 Walter Lippmann, *The Good Society* (New York: Grosset & Dunlap, 1943), 346.
6 John Hallowell, *The Moral Foundation of Democracy* (Chicago: The University of Chicago Press, 1954), 108.

But if it may thus be said that the principle of constitutionalism is disapproval of political power exercised for only particularistic ends, it is similar to the ultimate principle of morality itself. What is ethical conscience but the higher will in man which censures, and thereby defines, the arbitrary? Indeed, can it not be argued that to the extent that the principle of constitutionalism is not just the name for the flawed impartiality of enlightened self-interest, it is *identical* with ethical conscience? Clearly, whatever the apparent correspondence or proximity of self-interest and morality in some particular cases, man's ethical will is always in tension with the motive of selfishness. It cannot be said, therefore, that constitutionalism of every kind has moral worth. But as an activity by which men direct their common affairs, politics bears heavily on the achievement of the conditions of community. As such it is very much the concern of ethical conscience. What I am suggesting is that in one special sense constitutionalism is just another term for man's moral will applied to the organization of political activity. Constitutionalism is demanded by ethical conscience because it is necessary to the achievement of the moral goal. In its political aspect, the higher will may be called the spirit of constitutionalism. To develop this concept we need to remember that the words *government* and *constitution* are not names for something existing apart from the individual citizens. Those who participate in politics under the rules of a constitution accept it as a guide for their personal behavior, so that strictly speaking the constitution as a practical force is identical with the political activity of the individuals who assent to its provisions and supply or withold the spirit of constitutionalism.

If the good life is to be approached, men's lower inclinations have to be disciplined in some way. According to Edmund Burke, "Society requires not only that the passions of individuals should be subjected but that even in the mass and body, as well as in the individuals, the inclinations of men should frequently be thwarted, their will controlled, and their passions brought into subjection. This can only be done *by a power out of themselves*; and not, in the exercise of its function, subject to that will and to those passions which it is its office to bridle and subdue." [7] In its moral dimension this restraining power is in a certain sense external to individual persons as Burke writes. It transcends man. It is not a part of his lower self of unprincipled impulse, but disciplines it from the outside. But in another sense, which Burke does not here recognize, it is also *in* man. It is man's own ethical conscience, the principle of true humanity he shares with others.

The "private" habits by which the individual tries to lift himself out of the ever-present inclination to yield to morally unexamined impulse cannot be sharply distinguished from those of his habits which he tries to follow for the same purpose in his "public" or "political" life. They are, in fact, only two aspects of one and the same attempt to achieve the moral end. Since the end itself is social but its attainment dependent on individual effort, the prerequisites are both "private" and "public." In the "public" sphere, ethical conscience demands a special type of cooperation with others, namely one which minimizes the influence of arbitrariness. It applies to a political context a question which describes all moral deliberation: "Is this contemplated action good?" As entertained by the individual in politics, the same question may be formulated thus: "Is this contemplated 'public' action of the kind that contributes to community?" Although concerned with

---

7 Edmund Burke, *Reflections on the Revolution in France* (London: Everyman's Library, 1964), 57–58 (emphasis in original).

"public" affairs, it puts a moral obligation on each citizen.
The shared habit of asking this question is the moral dimension of constitutionalism. What should be carefully noted is
that this concern is translated by practical necessity into a
call for specific institutional restrictions binding on all. The
higher will in man does not work in a vacuum but on the concrete material of political reality. Given men's selfish and
otherwise flawed behavior and their unavoidable clashes of
interest, the political advancement of community is not possible without common assent to some superior coordinating
rule. The willingness to subject oneself to this kind of restraint out of concern for the moral end, therefore, is indistinguishable from ethical conscience itself. All actual constitutions are transcended by the ethical will, but the demand
for them is directly rooted in it. Applied to the conduct of
public affairs, thus, that will can indeed be described as the
spirit of constitutionalism.

In a democracy, constitutional provisions are imposed by
the people on itself. That does not mean that they will all
meet with the full approval of every citizen. While a person
may be critical of various parts of his country's constitution,
he may still respect it, *in the spirit of constitutionalism*. He may
recognize, in other words, that the continued curbing of
political arbitrariness requires of him that he should abide by
the provisions of which he disapproves as long as they are in
effect, and try to change them, not by stretching or otherwise
violating their meaning, but through the process of revision
prescribed by the constitution. He may also be on his guard
against the possibility that his own view of how the moral end
can be promoted by government is mistaken. In its denial of
all arbitrariness ethical conscience is a warning against premature certainty regarding the moral worthiness of concrete
political proposals. There is a crucial distinction to be made
between support for specific constitutional rules and the wil-

lingness itself to accept such rules, even when they may not seem wholly appropriate, in the interest of the higher goal.

Respect for the particular provisions of a constitution may be viewed as finally rooted in the intuition of a higher law, the approximation of which is understood to require the preservation of the dignity of man-made law. Thinking of constitutionalism as a "practical manifestation and reflection of the idea of natural law," Hallowell writes: "Constitutional government is a kind of self-restraint which the people in a democracy impose upon themselves; and, whether we have institutions of judicial review or not, its continued existence depends less upon the institutional checks provided than upon the commonly shared knowledge that there are restraints and upon willingness of individuals voluntarily to submit to those restraints." [8]

We may regard a constitution as forming a part of the varied cultural habits by which men direct their behavior towards the form of intrinsically valuable association which is community. These help to restrain the centrifugal, disruptive inclinations always present in society. They are tentative directives transcended by the directing principle itself. It is incompatible with the moral purpose of life to regard these habits as final, in need of no revision or improvement. The spirit of constitutionalism demands not only respect for the fundamental law, but the possibility to change that law on the basis of insight into how it could better serve the enduring goal. Particular constitutions are subject to a higher law. "To those who ask where this higher law is to be found," Walter Lippmann writes, "the answer is that it is a progressive discovery of men striving to civilize themselves, and that its scope and implications are a gradual revelation that is by no means completed." [9]

8 Hallowell, *Moral Foundation of Democracy*, 64.
9 Lippmann, *Good Society*, 347.

It has been one of my contentions that ethical conscience is better described as a principle of censure or self-examination than as a positive command to perform this or that act. Although moral conduct is attended by a sense of higher purpose, it never completely fulfills that purpose. The ultimate standard of good is always felt to have been betrayed to some extent. We may relate the idea of ethical conscience as a principle of censure to our discussion of constitutionalism by putting our own interpretation on the following compact statement by Calhoun: "It is, indeed, the *negative* power which makes the constitution, and the *positive* which makes the government. The one is the power of acting, and the other the power of preventing or arresting action. The two, combined, make constitutional governments." [10]

Against the background of the previous ethical analysis, these sentences may be read as a general description of man's moral life. The "negative power" would be the censuring, structuring activity of ethical conscience. The "positive power" we may understand as concrete human intentions. "The one is the power of acting," Calhoun writes, calling to mind our notion of impulse as the force which carries human action. The other is "the power of preventing or arresting action," he goes on, giving a description also of the role of ethical conscience in regard to impulse. "The two, combined, make constitutional governments." We may take that to mean that positive action, structured or disciplined by ethical conscience, is morality. This reading of the passage obviously strains Calhoun's meaning. He is referring in this statement not primarily to a moral "negative" on government. But since politics is largely the pursuit of partisan goals, the demands of ethical conscience in regard to the procedural rules tend to run parallel to those of enlightened self-interest. The moral

10 Calhoun, *Disquisition*, 28 (emphasis in original).

goal can be advanced only through a pragmatic adjustment to the stubborn reality of political self-seeking. In relation to the latter, ethical conscience has to be a "negative." The spirit of constitutionalism, as distinguished from actual constitutions, written or unwritten, is identical to ethical conscience as applied to the organization of political life; it advances community by seeking to curb political inclinations incompatible with that goal.

We are probably well-advised to pause briefly at this juncture to recapitulate some of our previous reasoning. This rendering of the relationship between ethical conscience and constitutionalism might seem to put an undue emphasis on the negative aspect of morality. Surely, morality also has a positive side. While this is certainly true, words must not take the place of precise analysis of the underlying meaning. I have explained before in some detail in what sense ethical conscience should be regarded as an "inner check," but to avoid misunderstanding in the present context a few additional remarks may be called for.

It might be objected that quick and spontaneous decisions are often moral, and that decisions based on careful deliberation could well be immoral. The latter part of the objection need not detain us, since it is simply a restatement of the position here presented: an attempt to protect deliberation through constitutional provisions may have no other motive than a morally oblivious wish to facilitate bargaining between factional groups. Constitutional restrictions in themselves are no guarantee that morality will be promoted.

But what about the other assertion, that spontaneous acts may sometimes be moral? First of all, it is lacking in clarity. If what is meant is that impulse somehow defines morality, it is clearly false, for particular intentions are always transcended by the ultimate standard of good. If what is meant, however, is that impulse may come to *participate* in and thus

advance the good, we are again entertaining a restatement of
our original position: ethical conscience gives its sanction to
certain impulses by withholding its censure and, as it were,
aligning itself with them.

Most likely, the mentioned objection is the result of skip-
ping over the essential question of just how impulses might
acquire moral worth. It is a failure to subject this question to
rigorous philosophical analysis which lends some credence to
Rousseauistic ethics. Leaving aside the case of spontaneity
which has moral consequences by mere chance, every moral
act is by definition sanctioned by ethical conscience. But as I
have argued at some length, that higher principle is itself
never identical to the impulse calling for action. The finite
reality of human acts is transcended by the good. In the
strictest sense, therefore, moral virtue is *always* associated
with a type of restraint. There is a never-ending tension between the imperfection of everything human and the standard
of perfection. Man is under a permanent censure which loses
some of its sharpness to the extent that he lives up to his
higher self. Ethical conscience is indeed a sense of purpose,
but in a world of flawed intentions and acts that purpose is
revealed either through censure or a qualified withholding of
censure. In the latter case, the specific act is attended by
moral reassurance.

If we say that spontaneous acts are sometimes moral, we
are describing in one highly ambiguous word what is in fact a
dualistic experience, namely impulse *and* the structuring role
of ethical conscience. The wording is acceptable only if it is
understood that what is called a spontaneous moral act is one
involving no *extended* ethical deliberation. Whether we take
as an example a person whose character has already been
morally structured, so that there is a certain moral momentum built into his impulsive life, or a situation in which the

moral course is so clear that there might be said to be an "impulsive" inclination to follow that course, it is only after an impulse has been arrested for ethical scrutiny, however quick, that the individual can recognize it as good and thus become justified to act on it. Moral conduct presupposes the interference of the question, "Is this moral?"—which is the particularized embodiment of ethical conscience. Aristotelian good habits, to illustrate, are neither spontaneously automatic nor compelled. They are the willing ordering of impulse toward a permanent goal.

This analysis in no way contradicts the idea that ethical conscience reveals a positive purpose. It is only a reminder that in relation to human finitude in general and human evil in particular this purpose is necessarily felt as an "inner check." This point deserves special emphasis in a discussion of constitutionalism, for politics is predominantly the pursuit of selfish interests. Moreover, although it is true that individual persons sometimes act morally "on impulse," a theory of democracy must concern itself with the question of how a certain type of *collective* activity is to be organized if it is to respect and promote the moral end.

If the spirit of constitutionalism is a rejection of the arbitrary, it is also an affirmation of the good life as it is advanced by politics. It negates *because* it affirms. To say that it demands institutional restraints on partisanship is to say that it promotes the moral opposite, the substance of which is the discovery of men trying to achieve community. In a certain sense, the moral end of society can be said to be undetermined; it is a goal that has to be pursued in changing circumstances. However, as the *spirit* in which political decisions ought to be made, that end is always the same. While it is impossible to outline once and for all the particulars of the good society, it can be defined in its political aspect as the

kind of society which is being realized when the people is acting in the spirit of constitutionalism. The belief that ethical
conscience sanctions positive acts by government is faultless.
But there is always a tendency among men of all political per-
suasions to exaggerate the moral purity of the cause they
happen to advocate. And even when the motive is pure, as far
as that is possible, the political wisdom of its translation into
practical proposals may be questionable. The spirit of constitutionalism responds to human imperfection and depravity on
the one hand, and the need for government action on the
other. As a constant reminder of man's shortcomings, it casts
a doubt on the moral worth of all political wishes. As an aspect of the principle of community, it is also what gives to
politics its higher direction and final justification.

I have rejected Rousseau's idea of plebiscitary democracy,
because it ignores the need for moral restraints in the individual and the people. Could it not be objected that what
is wrong with his democratic theory is not his rejection of
constitutionalism but his failure to recognize the need for
the moral self-discipline which could make his ideal of plebiscitary rule practicable? This is not really an objection to
my argument, but actually a somewhat confused confirma-
tion of it. Rousseau regards self-discipline in my sense of the
term as the very root of evil. Morality is served, he believes,
by uninhibited spontaneity. What should be understood is
that had he seen the moral necessity of self-restraint, he
would have had to drop his ban on constitutionalism. The
reason is that when men are engaging in political activity
under the type of restraints which are necessary if it is to
serve the common good, they are by that token also acting
constitutionally. The goal requires that they order their behavior with reference to a common standard not subject to
instantaneous repeal. The distinguishing mark of consti-

tutionalism is not so much the laying down of written provisions, as is the belief of Thomas Paine.[11] It is rather the
willingness for the sake of a higher goal to subject present
political wishes to scrutiny according to a set of rules not itself resting on the preference of the moment.

Just how maximum room is to be made for moral considerations in the making of government policy is a matter of applying the acceptance of restraints to difficult practical problems. The formulation of specific constitutional provisions,
including sanctions which increase the likelihood of adherence to them, has to be adjusted to the traditions and cultural
characteristics of the particular people. In a democracy, this
task is in the hands of the people and its representatives, the
implication being that the common good is best served by the
broadest possible participation in the process. Given the preponderance of selfish motives in politics, the goal of community cannot be advanced, except temporarily and by lucky
coincidence, by simply implementing the most recent expression of majority will. There is need for an element of pause,
of deliberation under the guidance of moral motives. Whatever the constitutional arrangements which are best designed
to encourage such an examination of intentions before they
can become government policy, those arrangements are demanded by ethical conscience.

11 According to Paine, wherever a constitution "cannot be produced in a visible
form, there is none. . . . Can then Mr. Burke produce the English Constitution? If he cannot, we may fairly conclude, that though it has been so much
talked about, no such thing as a constitution exists, or ever did exist, and consequently that the people have yet a constitution to form." Thomas Paine,
Rights of Man, ed. Henry Collins (Harmondsworth: Penguin Books, 1971),
93–94.

For some contrasting views of the nature of constitutionalism which are
closer to my own see, for instance, Charles H. McIlwain, *Constitutionalism
Ancient and Modern* (Ithaca: Cornell University Press, 1966), and Carl J.
Friedrich, *Constitutional Government and Democracy* (Waltham, Mass: Blais-
dell Publishing Co., 1968).

Constitutionalism versus Plebiscitarianism

It is not my purpose here to develop a set of constitutional prescriptions. I have used the American constitution to illustrate a general principle and not to assert that in the American context its provisions offer *the* practical solution to the problem of making democracy compatible with the needs of the ethical life. The Constitution does tend to restrain temporary popular majorities in a way conducive to the emergence of government by "consensus." It does so without giving tyrannical veto power to a self-seeking, dedicated minority. A majority which is not merely transitory and partisan, but capable of putting sustained or even mounting pressure on the various bodies of government, can overcome the resistance of a merely partisan minority. With its built-in premium on deliberation the United States Constitution provides an opportunity for putting ethical checks both on the people's representatives and on momentary electoral majorities.

We may gain some perspective on the moral necessity of constitutionalism and at the same time give more attention to the institutional problems of democracy by putting the American constitution alongside an old and recurrent criticism of that document which has given a strong element of ambiguity to the American political tradition. I am referring to a general impatience with representative institutions as set up by the Constitution. This dissatisfaction, which has marked plebiscitary overtones, is exemplified in the thought of Thomas Jefferson. In this Enlightenment figure of eclectic and often poorly integrated views one finds an unresolved strain, reflected in American politics to this day, between the constitutional temperament as understood in this discussion and a rather different temperament, more akin to that of Jean-Jacques Rousseau. It should be made clear that in concentrating for my purposes on Jefferson's strong plebiscitary tendency, I am not claiming to be analyzing more than one side of his thought. Not only are some of his arguments to which I will refer contradicted or modified by other of his statements, but it is also possible to argue that his theory was often contradicted by his practice.

Although Jefferson finally came around to endorsing the American constitution, one need not study his political thought for long to discover reasons for regarding his approval of constitutionalism in general as qualified and ambiguous. It should be noted at the outset that when Jefferson comes down most clearly on the side of constitutional restraints, as in the case of his insistence on a bill of rights, he is usually more concerned about protecting the people against their governors than the other way around. Although by no means blind to the shortcomings of the common man, his admitted inclination is to entrust the public interest to the mass of the people or a majority thereof rather than to popular representatives. It is significant that his democratic sentiments are of a kind that tends to undermine the principle of constitutionalism. He speaks of the ideal, regarded by him as unfortunately unattainable in practice, that "every form of government were so perfectly contrived, that the will of the majority could always be obtained, fairly and without impediment." The best available type of government, which he terms "re-

publican," is repeatedly described by him as one that allows
for the most direct and faithful execution of the people's will.
In its purest form, it would be "a government by its citizens
in mass, acting directly and personally, according to rules established by the majority." Negatively, the principle is stated
thus: "The further the departure from direct and constant
control by the citizens, the less has the government of the ingredient of republicanism." Jefferson's majoritarianism is
most clearly spelled out in his call for "absolute acquiscence
in the decisions of the majority—the vital principle of re-
publics." [1]

Jefferson's plebiscitary propensity brings him into collision
with the idea of representation developed by Edmund Burke
in his famous speech to his constituents in Bristol. Applying
this Burkean idea to democracy, we may take it to mean that
elected officials should not be mere executioners of shifting
popular wishes. The people should have the ultimate political
power, but the present majority should not have instant, un-
questioned authority to dictate government policy. Popular
representatives should have the opportunity to act independently to check and refine popular opinion. They should act
as the people's higher self. Jefferson, however, in many
places expresses deep suspicion of a conception of representation that might violate the principle of direct and immediate
popular control. He applauds a treatise on the American constitution by fellow Virginian John Taylor, which, in Jefferson's view, "settles unanswerably the right of instructing
representatives, and their duty to obey." Since direct popular
participation or control is impossible at the national level, Jefferson settles for "the nearest approach to a pure republic,

1 Thomas Jefferson, *The Life and Selected Writings of Thomas Jefferson*, ed. Ad-
rienne Koch and William Peden (New York: Modern Library, 1944), 492,
670, 324.

which is practicable," namely government through "representatives chosen either *pro hac vice*, or for such short terms as should render secure the duty of expressing the will of their constituents." [2]

Jefferson the plebiscitarian wants the removal of obstacles to the full and instant implementation of the people's will. Throughout he remains critical of important features in the Constitution which tend to thwart that goal. As might be expected, there is only one body in the national government of the United States that Jefferson is prepared to call "mainly republican" [3]—the House of Representatives. The reason is that, because the members of that body have a relatively short term of office, they can be expected to listen carefully to their constituents or else be rather promptly ousted. The Senate, the presidency, and the Supreme Court are all criticized by Jefferson for being too far removed from the control of the people, by the length of their terms of office or by the fact that they are chosen or appointed only indirectly by the people. What arouses his dissatisfaction is the very real possibility of a government policy which does not always meet with the approval of the majority. The logical extension of Jefferson's line of argument are such devices as recall and referendum, which have played some role in the American political tradition.

But perhaps the most striking example of Jefferson's anti-constitutional temperament is his belief that no country should go long without a revolution. "I hold it, that a little rebellion, now and then, is a good thing, and as necessary in the political world as storms in the physical." [4] At the bottom

---

2 *Ibid.*, 669, 670.
3 *Ibid.*, 671. I am relying in this paragraph primarily on Jefferson's illuminating letter to John Taylor of May 28, 1816.
4 *Ibid.*, 413.

of this lack of concern for the orderly process of government as a protection against arbitrariness lies a belief in the soundness or even goodness of the uninhibited popular will.

In view of the previous analysis of the relation between ethics and politics, it is not surprising that Jefferson's understanding of man should bear a strong resemblance in important respects to that of Rousseau. His view of human nature, like Rousseau's, is monistic. It comes in Jefferson's case steeped in an emphatic materialism and sensationalism.[5] Man's moral sense is not conceived by him as introducing a tension between immanent and transcendent in man's inner life. He describes it as a spontaneous force, an "instinct" which puts man on the moral course. Knowingly or unknowingly echoing Rousseau, he describes it as a pleasurable feeling of benevolence towards others which "prompts us irresistibly to feel and to succor their distresses."[6]

For Jefferson the plebiscitarian, we may state in conclusion, government does not have the purpose of restraining the momentary will of the people with a view to some higher moral standard. The wish of the majority at any moment is itself the most reliable expression of the public good. The best form of government is one which respects the principle that "the will of the majority is in all cases to prevail."[7]

The plebiscitary tendency in the American political tradition, contradicted in Jefferson's case by other elements, recurs in more recent expressions of impatience with constitutional restraints on the majority. A good example is the criticism directed against the so-called "deadlock of democracy" by James MacGregor Burns. The American constitu-

---

5 "On the basis of sensation, of matter in motion, we may erect the fabric of all the certainties we can have or need." *Ibid.*, 700. Jefferson's thinking in this as in many other respects is influenced by John Locke.

6 *Ibid.*, 638.

7 *Ibid.*, 322.

tional system, Burns complains, is defective in that it "requires us to await a wide consensus before acting." It will not allow the speedy and effective implementation of the will of the majority, which should be the purpose of democracy. The basis of the presumption against simple majority rule in the Constitution, Burns observes, "has been a pervading distrust of the people when organized in a national block or party. The people, yes—but only in their separated, federalized, localized capacities. Popular government, yes—but not really popular rule by hungry majorities." The latter kind of government ought to be established, Burns argues, by revising the American form of government in accordance with what he calls "the Jeffersonian model." This model he draws from Jefferson the practical politician, whom he regards as wedded to the ideal of vigorous government action supported by a national majority coalition. Jeffersonian majority rule, Burns contends, has "a more popular, egalitarian impetus than the Madisonian." [8] Burns proposes several reforms designed to create a new form of government, such as abolition of the Electoral College, federal control over elections to the national government, making congressional districts more uniform, removal of procedures which discourage popular voting, centralization of the political parties, and removal of traditional congressional practices which undermine party discipline. What he wants is a system in which decisive power belongs to the numerical national majority and in which political candidates are members of national parties with distinct, well-defined platforms, so that elections can in effect become national plebiscites on alternative government policies.

What is of immediate concern to us here are not the specific reforms suggested by Burns, but the temperament that

8 James MacGregor Burns, *The Deadlock of Democracy* (Englewood Cliffs, N.J.: Prentice-Hall, 1963), 323, 334–35, 41.

inspires them. According to Burns, the majority principle
joined to a system of national party competition is not enough
to make possible the sweeping governmental action that must
be available to the majority in a more democratic America. It
will take determined, central leadership. The decisive role
must be played by the president. He must "assume full responsibility, in the priority areas, for the functions and effectiveness of the whole governmental system." When the power
of the presidency "is exercised most responsibly it is not
confined to mere tinkering." [9] The man holding that office
must be able and willing to cut through the separation-of-
powers apparatus in order to get things done. For example,
he has to "ignore the absurd 'rule' . . . that the President
does not interfere in the legislative department. He must interfere, and openly so." In his approving analysis of Jefferson's leadership in broadening executive power on the basis
of a mobilized national majority, Burns observes: "The high
point of Jefferson's majoritarianism . . . came in the Louisiana Purchase. When the chips were down, when a great decision had to be made and pressed quickly, Jefferson violated
congressional rights, by-passed accepted constitutional processes, refused to go through the long process of a constitutional amendment, and threw himself and his party on
the mercy of the new popular majority that he was building up." [10]

Whatever the accuracy of this interpretation of Jefferson's
action, it is apparent that Burns sees a need for executive
leadership that is willing to bend or even break the rules
when it is necessary to serve the presumed interests of the
majority. "The great political leader is not content to whittle

9 James MacGregor Burns, *Uncommon Sense* (New York: Harper & Row, 1972),
   129, 173.
10 Burns, *Deadlock of Democracy*, 338, 39–40.

down his goals to what he thinks he can achieve through the existing structure of political forces. Rather he seeks to enlarge and vivify the structure so that the goals can be realized as fully as possible. He knows that archaic governmental routines cannot always be broken up by adjustment and adaptation but . . . by 'the application of overwhelming external force.'" [11]

Burns's impatience with constitutional obstacles to instant and sweeping change does not quite amount to a repudiation of the idea of constitutionalism. Whether for tactical or other reasons, he does not attack it head on. But he undermines it by advocating an exercise of power not overly sensitive to the intent or spirit of constitutional provisions. If he sees the danger of political arbitrariness, he is apparently less disturbed by it than by the risk that the popular majority might not get its way.

It has been suggested by critics that Burns's unwillingness to accept the restraints of the American constitution is rooted in frustration over the fact that at this time in American history those restraints happen to reduce the likelihood of public implementation of the particular policies that he believes to be mandatory. [12] Assuming, however, that his arguments for the empowering of numerical national majorities is not just a case of intellectual opportunism, we must take him to mean that there is something about the uninhibited will of the mass of the people which entitles it to a decisive influence over government policy. If Burns is to retain the idea that democracy can be defended on ethical grounds, the presumption must be that this type of popular will is somehow morally

11 Burns, *Uncommon Sense*, 175.
12 Willmoore Kendall writes, for instance: "Since Burns and his friends *cannot* win under the existing rules, he asks us to change the rules so that he and his friends *can* win." *Contra Mundum*, ed. Nellie D. Kendall (New Rochelle, N.J.: Arlington House, 1971), 273 (emphasis in original).

superior to other types. He would be leaning then in the direction of the Rousseauistic belief in the morality of spontaneous popular wishes as they emerge, not from citizens in their capacity as members of social groups, but in their capacity as members of the undifferentiated mass. Although Rousseau does not advocate strong executive leadership by one individual for normal circumstances, it is difficult not to see the affinity between his pervasive hostility to inner and outer restraints and Burns's belief that "the presidency at its best seeks to liberate American society as a whole from whatever binds it." [13] The premise at work would seem to be that only if the people is free to cast off all institutional shackles can true democracy be realized.

It would be possible to question the democratic claims of Burns's brand of plebiscitarianism by arguing that it enhances the danger of popularly supported despotism, or "Caesarism" in James Burnham's term. [14] The United States Constitution as it now stands implies a wide variety of sectional and local associations and attachments among the people. It might be said that the Constitution assumes the most significant meaning of "the people" to be the citizens organized in groups of various kinds. Contrary to the Rousseauistic ideal, it does not expect the citizens to disregard their membership in such associations when addressing public issues. The sense of the people is taken, not so much with reference to their mere numbers as their concrete, social natures. What is desired is that a concern for the welfare of one's own associations be joined to or at least tempered by a concern for the good of the people as a whole. A constitution that protects and also en-

---

13 Burns, *Uncommon Sense*, 173.
14 *Cf.* James Burnham, *Congress and the American Tradition* (Chicago: Henry Regnery Co., 1965), especially Chap. 25. See also Peter Viereck, *The Unadjusted Man* (Westport, Conn.: Greenwood Press, 1973), Chap. 15.

courages sectional and local associations and a general decentralization and dispersion of power is among other things a
potent obstacle against attempts to mobilize a people behind
the man on horseback. Apart from the institutional hurdles
sanctioned in law, citizens who have close ties to various social groups are not likely to give their undivided loyalty to a
political leader or organization. One general effect of Burns's
proposed institutional reforms, however, would seem to be to
promote the transformation of the American people "in their
separated, federalized, localized capacities" into something
closer to the Rousseauistic ideal of an undifferentiated mass
of individuals. Burns's wish is that the will of the people be
determined with reference to the numerical national majority. One wonders if the institutional detachment or dissolu-
tion of the people which will make this possible does not also
make easier the task of a tyrannical majority or a despotic
popular leader who in the name of the people would like to establish complete political control. It is worthy of note that insistence on the unlimited authority of the popular will often
tends to go together with a preference for highly centralized,
or even totalitarian, forms of government.

Although not entirely clear-cut, Burns's theory of democracy exhibits a general tendency whose ultimate ethical and
political implications are brought out in the thought of Jean-
Jacques Rousseau. Burns and other theorists of democracy of
the plebiscitary bent may not actually be self-admitted disciples of Rousseau and, needless to say, they are likely to differ
with him in many particulars. They do share with him an
impatience with constitutional restraints and a related presumption in favor of the spontaneous popular will. In the
final analysis, their type of democratic theory must be defended on moral grounds. They may not all have recognized
the full implications of their plebiscitary preferences, but the

logical ethical basis for those preferences is supplied by Rousseau. And if my analysis of that archetypal plebiscitarian is generally correct, they do not withstand critical examination. We are justified, therefore, in approaching the institutional prescriptions of these theorists with considerable skepticism.

A theory of democracy which does not recognize the paramount need of constitutionalism evades the realities of man's moral predicament. An attempt to carry the plebiscitary ideal into practice will tend, in the long run at least, to defeat the ethical purpose of community and thereby also to undermine popular rule itself. Plebiscitary democracy, it may be suggested, is not really a political concept at all, but a quasi concept. It is not based on a realistic assessment of the possibilities open to man, but on some highly dubious assumptions: *assuming* that political man is not predominantly or even partially motivated by selfishness; *assuming* that he is instead spontaneously propelled in the direction of morality; *assuming* that the popular majority of the moment is most likely to give expression to the common good—assuming all of this, plebiscitary democracy becomes a concept descriptive of human potentiality. But these things, I have tried to show, cannot be assumed. They actually run counter to concrete experience. Few modern democratic theorists embrace plebiscitarianism in the pure Rousseauistic form, but many lean in that direction. To that extent they give to democratic theory a utopian slant inimical to a realistic consideration of the institutional problems of popular rule.

That is not to say that each proposal for changing the American political system which is advanced by thinkers like Burns is necessarily destructive of the moral goal of politics. Precisely what constitutional arrangements will help to make democracy compatible with the needs of the ethical life under some particular historical circumstances is not just a matter of motive but of political prudence and imagination. Obviously, constitutional restraints are not an end in themselves. They are desirable insofar as they serve the higher goal. For many reasons even the most nobly and skillfully conceived constitution may at some time begin to defeat its original purpose. Profound social and political changes may necessitate constitutional amendment or even transformation. A sound constitution recognizes that fact and provides the means for its own revision. The point to be made about Burns's recommendations is that whatever merit may be found in them attaches to them not because of, but in spite of, his plebiscitary leanings.

This argument regarding the two available concepts of popular rule may perhaps be summed up by drawing a parallel between two types of citizens and two types of democracy. Rousseau asks us to picture an individual who always acts spontaneously. To this type of citizen corresponds a form of democracy which gives complete freedom to the spontaneous popular will. This plebiscitary notion of democracy is not founded in reality but in an utopian world. We may oppose to this another image, which pictures an individual who acts under self-imposed moral restraints. To that kind of citizen corresponds a popular government under constitutional limitations designed to promote a certain quality of popular will. Only this type of democracy recognizes man's real moral predicament. It allows an opportunity to temper the forces of political self-seeking by considerations of the common good. It can be joined to and sustained by man's sense of higher purpose. Constitutional democracy at its best, we may conclude, would be popular self-rule in the cause of community. To the extent that democracy approaches this high standard, it can be supported on moral grounds. Going a step further than is really warranted by my argument, it may perhaps even be said that in this concept of democracy we have the noblest idea of politics.

Decentralization

Because I have sought to relate ethical conscience to institutions of government and used the American constitution as a practical illustration, it might perhaps be inferred that I am putting considerable faith in the potential of a large society like the United States to become a community as here defined. This implication is not intended. It should be understood that my theory of the reconciliation of popular rule with the ethical life is not restricted to any particular level of government. Indeed, the spirit of constitutionalism is the political aspect of a principle which applies to all forms of associated activity. The thesis is not so much that there can be a "national" community; it is rather that *to the extent* that community can be promoted by government at whatever level, the latter must be guided by the spirit of constitutionalism.

It has been persuasively argued by many theorists that the element of conflict in life tends to grow as you move from local to national relationships, and from national to international.[15] My theory of democracy is not intended to contradict this view, as long as it is understood that concepts like *local, national*, and *international* are not philosophically distinct categories but only pragmatically useful classifications. We cannot expect the cessation of the war of all against all. The motive of community is forever threatened by mere partisanship. National politics, even more than local politics, is

15 See, for example, Reinhold Niebuhr, *Moral Man and Immoral Society* (New York: Charles Scribner's Sons, 1960), Hans Morgenthau, *Politics Among Nations* (New York: Alfred A. Knopf, 1959), and Raymond Aron, *Peace and War* (New York: Praeger, 1967).

likely to exhibit a weak impetus toward morality. Still, to the extent that a people is able to transcend selfish interests, it is making its government a partial manifestation of community.

One conclusion of my whole argument is that community could not exist in an undifferentiated mass of individuals. It consists in a special type of associated activity. The argument has not been designed to prove, but has nevertheless hinted, that the values of true community are most likely to be realized in groups which are much less than socially all-encompassing. This theme has been developed with great care and perceptiveness by Robert Nisbet.[16] He argues convincingly that it is in the "autonomous groups" of society, such as the family, the local church, school, and club, that most men will be able to find a sense of meaningful belonging and personal worth. A feeling of community thrives in associations of small, manageable proportions. This line of argument raises a very important question which is intimately related to the one I have sought to answer in this study: must not democracy, if it is to be conducive to truly human values, keep the control over public decisions as close as possible to those who are affected by them? Here, it may be possible to find some considerable common ground with contemporary political theorists whose philosophical premises are quite different from my own. Looking for ways to counteract the powerlessness induced by big government (and big organizations generally) in today's Western democracies, Robert Dahl, for example, suggests the following as one "pragmatic principle": "If a matter is best dealt with by a democratic association, seek always to have that matter dealt with by the smallest association that can deal with it satisfactorily."[17]

16 Nisbet's position is summarized in *Community and Power* (New York: Oxford University Press, 1962).
17 Robert Dahl, *After the Revolution?* (New Haven: Yale University Press, 1970), 102.

One need not endorse Dahl's entire political theory or all of his institutional recommendations to accept this idea, which looks much like a rediscovery in modern circumstances of the classical idea of subsidiarity. The evidence about the conditions of community that has been presented, together with that supplied by scholars like Nisbet, indicates that Dahl's principle, which is of course not original with him among contemporary thinkers, is a necessary supplement to my own theory of democracy. If community does require decentralized government and vital autonomous groups, as seems indeed to be the case, it is obvious that the formulation of particular democratic constitutions must be adjusted to this need. My own contribution is the thesis that, whatever the level or scope of government, its activities must reflect the spirit of constitutionalism if community is to be promoted. This is not to assume that the "nation" is the primary sphere of community. Actually, my position coincides with Burke's view that the source of warm feelings for the state as a whole is in the affections that we develop for the smaller groups to which we belong in society.

"Democratization"

According to some contemporary theorists, the time has come to extend democratic decision making to areas of social life which have long been regarded as belonging to the "private" sphere—for example, the business corporation. In the United States, arguments of this kind have been advanced by Robert Dahl and Peter Bachrach. The issue is too large to be dealt with adequately here, but a few brief remarks may help to clarify my own main point. It should be obvious from the rejection of a sharp distinction between "public" and "private" that I am not inclined to accept the type of rigid, aprioristic notion of the proper role of government which is found in some socialists, laissez-faire liberals, and anarchists. By the same token, I could only be suspicious of the view that the salvation of modern democracy is in a broader application of a certain method of making decisions. With somewhat different emphases, Dahl and Bachrach contend that we are employing a too restrictive conception of what falls in the "political" category.[18] Significantly, the two men appear to be guilty of precisely the same mistake in that they treat democracy as primarily a set of formal rules. Theirs would seem to be a procedural view of popular government, only one with a majoritarian and egalitarian slant, strongest perhaps in Bachrach. It is symptomatic that Dahl is forced to speak of certain types of delegated political authority that he himself believes are necessary to effective popular rule as "nondemocratic."[19] Lacking in both theorists is a clear understanding of the difference between plebiscitary and constitutional democracy and of the fact that democracy, if it is to be a meaningful idea, must be viewed as implying a whole way of life.

Political institutions are indistinguishable from the cultural ethos of a people. Therefore, if a society is losing its commitment to what is above short-term economic efficiency and various kinds of narrow self-interest, the introduction of a certain decision-making device into new areas is not likely to lead to a restoration of genuine human values. The argument of Dahl and Bachrach is refreshing in that it challenges the conventional liberal and socialistic views of the role of the state. For the most part, however, the two men do not go beyond a new combination of these views under the guiding principle of "more democracy"—to which one may say with Irving Babbitt that what is needed is not more, but better

18 See Dahl, *After the Revolution?* and Peter Bachrach, *The Theory of Democratic Elitism* (Boston: Little, Brown and Company, 1967).
19 Dahl, *After the Revolution?*, 88–98.

democracy.[20] The problem of finding the institutional means through which the good society can be promoted in new circumstances is most certainly a very important one. It should be faced in a pragmatic frame of mind, and the magnitude of the difficulties confronting democracy today may well require some unorthodox solutions. The prerequisite of truly well-considered proposals, however, is an understanding of the nature of community. Much of the present concern about the undermining of democracy in modern Western society does spring from a sense that essential human values are increasingly threatened. Unfortunately, when it comes to showing what, ultimately, is a human value, most modern democratic theory is sadly lacking. In this area various doctrines of moral relativism or nihilism are a major obstacle to intellectual renewal. As long as this fundamental flaw persists, the institutional reforms that are suggested will all too often be desperate shots in the dark. It is not enough to insist, as is fashionable among social scientists today, that once again "values" have to be taken into account or promoted by scholars. What is needed in democratic theory is not some infusion of subjectively derived "value preferences" in the spirit of plebiscitarianism, but an effort to rethink the problems of popular government in the light of the transcendent standard of community.

20 Irving Babbitt, *Democracy and Leadership* (New York: Houghton Mifflin Co., 1924).

Democracy, Leadership, and Culture

If popular rule without effective constitutional restraints is an ethically unacceptable notion, popular rule under such restrictions offers no guarantee that moral motives will be promoted. Constitutional restraints are a necessary but not sufficient condition for the furtherance of community. Everything turns on the absence or presence of what I have called the spirit of constitutionalism. It will emerge only in a people of advanced spiritual culture.

Referring to the United States but making a general observation, René de Visme Williamson argues that "the Constitution functions as a mirror for the national conscience." [1] The constitutional norm serves as a constant reminder of the contrast between the values endorsed by the people in its better moments, when it looks at politics in the perspective of the moral end, and the imperfect, sometimes degrading practice of day-to-day politics. The law thus has a moral function. John Middleton Murry writes, "Just as the democratic society freely chooses its government, so the democratic citizen must freely choose to do his duty to the commonweal. He puts his conscience in control of his actions. He obeys the law, not as an external command, but as the expression of his

---

1 René de Visme Williamson, *Independence and Involvement* (Baton Rouge: Louisiana State University Press, 1964), 126–27.

own better self, which wills to act in obedience to a law
which its reason recognizes to be necessary." [2]

Representative institutions, which are central to any constitutional system, do not by themselves assure the moral
dignity of democratic politics. The people must be not only
able to recognize but also willing to give their support to leaders who have a genuine concern for the common good. That
presupposes a measure of moral attainment and perspicacity
as well as trust. According to Williamson, "People who have
no ideals can have no representatives." [3] Representation in
the morally significant sense implies a shared understanding
of the ultimate goal of life and also an awareness that some
men are better equipped for leadership than others. The true
criterion is not wealth, position, or birth, but a special type of
ability. The good representative is able to represent not the
lower, partisan selves of his fellow citizens, but their will to
community. The willingness to put this kind of trust in
elected leaders, to the point of respecting their judgment
when it goes contrary to one's own wishes of the moment, is
essential to the fulfillment of the higher goal of democracy.
To be worthy of such trust, a popular representative cannot
be just an average, ordinary person. In addition to prudence
and skill, he should have in even greater measure than those
who elect him a sense of the moral purpose of politics. In a
position to lead and not follow only, he ought to be able to rise
above the popular passions and biases of the hour and even of
his own period in history.

Let there be no hedging or equivocation on this point: constitutional democracy implies and requires leadership. Contrary to various utopian dreams, every possible form of gov-

---

2 John Middleton Murry, "The Moral Foundation of Democracy," *Fortnightly*
(September, 1947), 168.
3 Williamson, *Independence and Involvement*, 198.

ernment will have its "elites." The democratic ideal is not to
do away with leaders, but to make them as numerous as possible and to create the circumstances in which a commitment
to the common good is encouraged among them. John Hallowell rightly observes, "It is not a characteristic feature of
democracy that it dispenses with authority; that is, instead,
characteristic of tyranny. There can be no freedom without
authority, for without authority freedom degenerates into
license." [4]

Here, constitutionalism plays an important role. It places
restraints on the inclination to misuse power both among
elected leaders and the electorate. These restrictions, however, become morally effective only if they form part of a
whole pattern of high aspirations in the people. Reinhold
Niebuhr recognizes the importance of moral culture when he
writes:

While political strategies deal with outer and social checks upon
the egoism of men and of nations and while no individual or collective expression of human vitality is ever moral enough to obviate the
necessity of such checks, it is also true that outer checks are in-
sufficient if some inner moral checks upon human ambition are not
effective. Consistently egoistic individuals would require a tyrannical government for the preservation of social order. Fortunately individuals are not consistently egoistic. Therefore democratic government, rather than Thomas Hobbes' absolutism, has proved a
possiblity in national life. [5]

The emergence and maintenance of an elevated general
sense as to the proper end of the political order requires both
assimilation of mankind's noblest spiritual traditions and
creativity in their application to new circumstances. Political

4 John Hallowell, *The Moral Foundation of Democracy* (Chicago: The University
of Chicago Press, 1954), 119.
5 Reinhold Niebuhr, *The Children of Light and the Children of Darkness* (New
York: Charles Scribner's Sons, 1960), 182.

morality is dependent on what is contributed by upbringing and education in the family, by schools and universities, churches, authors and artists, and, as important as anything else, the personal example of good men. Apart from prudential and intellectual virtues, the citizens and their representatives in a democracy must have some commitment to the morally mandatory, although never fully attainable, goal of community. In the Western world, we are heavily indebted for our understanding of this supreme social value and its prerequisites to the classical and Judaeo-Christian tradition. Christianity, especially, with its inclusive view of who are to contribute to and participate in community has provided indispensable support for popular government. By giving his ultimate loyalty to a cause which transcends his own time and place and the merely partisan wishes of his own people, the democratic citizen does not betray the idea of popular self-rule, but, on the contrary, affirms the unifying principle which alone can sustain it in the long run and give it moral worth.

True leadership, like the spirit of constitutionalism, is incompatible with spiritual arrogance. Although the popular representative must in a sense seek to put himself above his constituents, the proper standard for so doing puts even his best efforts in a humbling light. Criticizing various humanitarian "uplifters" who take a certain arrogant pleasure in caring for the underdog, Irving Babbitt writes: "A man needs to look, not down, but up to standards set so much above his ordinary self as to make him feel that he is himself spiritually the underdog. The man who thus looks up is becoming worthy to be looked up to in turn, and, to this extent, qualifying for leadership." [6]

6 Irving Babbitt, *Democracy and Leadership* (New York: Houghton Mifflin Co., 1924), 257.

A sense of the contrast between man's true destiny, as reflected in the highest standards of conduct known by civilization, and man's actual behavior is inseparable from all morally authoritative leadership. This qualification, it should be emphasized, has particular application to democracy, for in that form of government each adult is supposed to be to some extent a leader of others. The simultaneous awareness of human limitations and potentialities, which grows out of several thousand years of spiritual experience and intellectual effort, is also the very root of constitutionalism in the higher sense. We subject our political conduct to the restraints of a common legal authority, because we know that premature certainty, self-seeking, and even positive evil always threaten to infect our actions. Pledging to respect a constitution conceived with concern for the common good, we recognize both our depravity and our sacred destiny.

PART FIVE

A Postscript

The Common Good and History

This book has sought to determine to what extent and in what form democracy is compatible with the ethical imperative of human existence. In arguing for a fundamental distinction between constitutional and plebiscitary democracy and demonstrating the ethical deficiency of the latter, it has set forth a general understanding of the way in which the transcendent moral order affects politics. To the extent that politics is influenced by ethical conscience, it helps to build up the common good, a quality of life to which one may also refer, stressing its more intimate form, as community. The meaning of the common good, as related to the circumstances of democracy, can be clarified by addressing some possible objections to the previous argument.

Four closely related lines of reasoning may be restated and extended. First, it is a source of possible puzzlement or unease that ethical universality has not been identified with specific principles of right. What is ultimately normative in the ethical life is not a form of rationality but a special quality of will. Ethical good does not result from imitating a preexisting intellectual model. The ethical authority to which man finally defers is a higher purposiveness within practical experience. This higher will is a power within the particular person, but it is not under the control of the individual in the sense that he can arbitrarily decree what is good. Still, the ethical purpose of the higher will must be realized in the particular circumstances of those who act under its authority. Although reason is indispensable to this effort, it is misguided to look for "principles" of conduct that are valid at all times and in all places. The ethical life does need norms to help orient human action to its higher end, but all specific rules of guidance are transcended by the ethical needs of actual situations. Advancing the common good in politics is not a matter of formulating an ethical master plan and implementing it by central direction. Discerning opportunities for good is not a monopoly of singularly enlightened individuals or groups. Laws and other forms of direction are necessary to the good society, but even the most comprehensive and best-laid plans are defied by the complexity and variability of life.

Second, it will raise questions that the understanding of ethical universality here propounded does not contrast the particular interests of individuals, groups and associations with a disinterested common good. It is contended instead that all of human existence, including the ethical life, is a pursuit of interests. Disinterested life is a contradiction in terms. So is politics without partisanship. Without a readiness to contend with competing interests, nothing can be achieved. A purpose not carried by the energy of will does not belong to the world of action. Ethical universality can be advanced only through the particular aspirations of ethically interested individuals and groups who assert their will against contrary interests.

Third, this book argues that no society can expect to derive the order it needs solely or primarily from the ethical aspirations of its citizens. Since the moral flaws of human nature are considerable and inescapable, personal and social order must be derived in part from man's lower desires. This is pos-

sible because selfishness contains within itself a great capacity for self-control, discipline being in the long run more conducive to its interests than a lack thereof. An ethically very
important goal of constitutional arrangements is to make selfishness less rash and blatant, to give it reasons to be more
enlightened. Out of concern for its own long-term advantage,
selfishness may, under institutional inducements, begin to accommodate other interests in society, and among them interests of ethical inspiration. To that extent, enlightened selfishness is bent, however modestly, to the purposes of the ethical
life. It may even offer some unintended support for the common good in the ethical sense.

   Fourth, ethics as here understood does not indulge in wish-
ful thinking. It does not entertain the possibility of eradicating egotism from human life, especially not from politics. The
ethical life must seek its opportunities in an often inhospit-
able environment. It must recognize its own limited power
and adjust its means to the stubborn obstacles it faces. The
ethical spirit of constitutionalism can be said to accept interests at odds with the common good, not in the sense of approving them but in the sense of acknowledging their inevitability.
Immoral forces form part of the frequently discouraging material out of which means must be forged for promoting the
common good. The ethical will works on life as it actually is
to change it for the better. It continually adjusts to selfishness, making use of it for its own ends as opportunities present themselves. The higher will achieves concrete, if sometimes very limited, good. This ethical realism, consisting of
correspondence between means and concrete circumstances,
may be contrasted with espousal of allegedly high but abstract
principles. A disembodied moralism of that sort makes ethics
ineffectual and even irrelevant by separating it from mundane
concrete situations. It is necessary to question the morality of

a moral idealism that does not predispose the individual to looking for and seizing moral opportunities actually at hand.

For those who deny the existence of a universal standard of good, suggesting the ethical inferiority or superiority of any political and social arrangements is objectionable. To many people who claim to accept such a standard, on the other hand, the view of ethics and politics just outlined will seem too vague and ambiguous. Does not ethics in politics presuppose the existence of definite, clear principles of right discernible by reason, a kind of blueprint for the good society and individual human action? Unless the proper goal for human striving is somehow already defined, how could one know in what direction to steer society, know whether it is improving or deteriorating? Associating the pursuit of the common good with continuous adjustment to changing situations would appear to leave man at the mercy of shifting historical circumstances. And must not true ethical universality be wholly free of particular interests? What is a common good composed of particular interests but an unstable coalition of selfish factions? And what could be more destructive of the idea of ethics in politics than dwelling on life's moral imperfections and their intractability, and, even worse, permitting these considerations to enter into the very definition of the ethical? Such a way of thinking appears to compromise the higher good in politics and to settle for unacceptably modest expectations. The real standard of political good, so the objection may be summarized, must be not only definite and specific and knowable by reason but elevated far above the indignities of our changeable historical existence.[1]

1   The kind of ethical rationalism that is here criticized is represented by large numbers of philosophers and political thinkers ranging from Thomists and Neo-Thomists to secular exponents of ahistorical ethical principles or natural rights. For two fairly representative examples from political thought that are also quite

The Particularity of Ethical Good

These concerns may be addressed by expanding and making more explicit some parts of the understanding of ethical universality that informs this book. It may be helpful to relate the ideas of constitutional democracy and the common good to the philosophical position of value-centered historicism. It needs to be explained further that the ethical imperative, while it transcends the particularities of history, is also a power within history. As such, it becomes immanent in concrete particulars. What is propounded is a historicized notion of ethical universality and the political common good. Contrary to a widespread assumption, interpreting the transcendent as potentially immanent in history does not threaten its ethical integrity or obliterate it as a guide for human life. The opposite is true. It is the possible inherence of ethical universality in particular circumstances themselves that gives it a vital relationship to human affairs. It is the variability of its concrete substance that guarantees its relevance and effectiveness in perpetually changing circumstances.[2]

To insist on an ahistorical conception of ethical universality is to separate the ordering power from the world in which we

---

different in many respects, see Heinrich Rommen, *The State in Catholic Thought* (New York: Greenwood Press, 1969), and Leo Strauss, *Natural Right and History* (Chicago: University of Chicago Press, 1953). Needless to say, ethical rationalism can be more or less abstract and ahistorical. Some thinkers who use the language of "law," "rights," or "reason" to refer to ethical universality actually come close, in substance, to the idea of a higher will and to a historical understanding of ethical universality. See, for example, Peter Stanlis, *Edmund Burke and the Natural Law* (Ann Arbor: University of Michigan Press, 1965), and Walter Lippmann, *The Public Philosophy* (New York: New American Library, 1956). For an attempt to modify ethical rationalism and build a historical dimension into Aristotelianism, see Alasdair MacIntyre, *After Virtue,* second edition (Notre Dame: University of Notre Dame Press, 1984).

2 The philosophical position of value-centered historicism is explicated, with emphasis on its epistemological foundation, in Claes G. Ryn, *Will, Imagination and Reason* (Chicago and Washington, D.C.: Regnery Books, 1986).

live. It is the *denial* of the possible synthesis of the universal
and the particular that undermines the integrity and relevance of ethical universality. It is true that an abstract model
of the good society that is formulated by a thinker of great
ethical sensibility and wisdom may convey some of the universality of purpose of the real ethical imperative. But turning
ethical universality into an intellectual blueprint creates an
ultimately unbridgeable gap between the alleged norm and
the concrete needs of historical situations. Real universality,
by contrast, is embodied in particular actions that meet those
needs.

The deeply ingrained intellectual habit of separating ethical
universality from the specifics of man's historical existence
has many unfortunate practical and theoretical consequences. One of them is that terms like "virtue," "justice,"
"right," and "the common good," as divorced from any concrete experiential content, become vacuous and highly elas-
tic. They are easily made to accommodate opposites. Ahistorical ethical rationalism has some relevance and credibility
only because those contemplating the meaning of its concepts
actually read into them particular experiential referents. Abstract notions of ethical philosophy are belied by philosophical
practice. As against an ahistorical perspective on ethics and
politics, it is contended here that real ethical universality reveals its nature only in the concrete actions that advance its
purpose. The essence of the ethical is discovered not in an
abstract, disembodied sphere beyond human action but in
particular, historical manifestations.

The importance of understanding universality in this manner may be demonstrated with reference to the ethics of popular government. It has been argued that the structures of
constitutional democracy are potentially conducive to man's
higher purpose, whereas plebiscitary democracy tends to defeat the ethical life. That is to say that ethical universality

manifests itself in certain patterns of action that exclude
other patterns. What should be noted is that these behavioral
biases *embody* the purpose of the ethical life, reveal its distinctive nature and objective in particular political circumstances. Apart from concrete manifestations such as these,
terms chosen to designate what is ethical in politics are vacuous and susceptible to theoretical manipulation.

The distinction between constitutional and plebiscitary democracy expresses two sharply different understandings of
man's moral nature. Just as the term "ethical universality"
acquires real meaning only as connected with particular patterns of action, so "democracy" acquires real meaning only as
connected with concrete particulars. The two forms of democracy are not two versions of a single type. They entail
sharply different institutions and imply sharply contrasting
views of human nature and society. Their respective ethical
substances clash. If the word democracy is used for both in
deference to conventional usage and to indicate a preference
for popular consent, this terminological similarity is mislead-
ing insofar as it seems to indicate a deeper affinity between
the two forms. Constitutional and plebiscitary democracy signify orientations that are actually destructive of each other.

Constitutional democracy, to summarize some of its concrete substance, sees the need for restraints on the popular
will of the moment. It adopts representative and other institutions with the aim of encouraging and articulating the
higher wishes of the people. Constitutional democracy understands by a people citizens associated in groups of a more or
less intimate kind whose lives are shaped and whose interests
are expressed largely through these groups. This form of government is conducive to a proliferation of intermediate, autonomous associations and to limited, decentralized political
power. Plebiscitary democracy exists nowhere in pure form,

but it aspires to the Rousseauistic ideal of unrestricted rule by the numerical majority. The people's momentary wishes should dictate policy. The notion of a people that corresponds to plebiscitary democracy is the undifferentiated mass of individuals. This form of government favors the large collective over local and private associations and fosters a centralization and expansion of government.

Uncritically examined, these forms of popular government may appear to have much in common—for example, acceptance of popular sovereignty, electoral competition, broad suffrage, and government responsible to voters. But the concrete reality of such institutions and practices may diverge drastically. Their substance depends on the role they play in the larger whole and on the character and purpose of the individuals who act through them. It has been shown previously that "popular sovereignty" can have very dissimilar meanings. The same is true of "people," "popular consent," and other terms. Popular voting may be practiced by a deracinated, undifferentiated mass of people or by citizens rooted in vital communities. It can reflect the passions of the moment or well-considered, deliberate opinion. Voting can give expression to blatantly partisan interests or to responsible efforts to advance the common good. Government officials can serve the people by demagogically promising benefits without cost or by pursuing unpopular but necessary policies.

These are not examples of the same institutions being used for varying ends. Human institutions are not inert objects external to specific human aspirations, like containers that may hold miscellaneous fluids without themselves changing. Form and substance are indistinguishable. The substance of institutions is constituted by particular actions. As action serves different ultimate ends it creates different institutions.

It needs to be underlined that the institutions of constitutional democracy as here understood are entirely dependent on the preponderance in society of a particular character type. Plebiscitary democracy assumes the preponderance of another kind of citizen. If a constitutional democracy should begin to be dominated by the latter type of individual, it is in effect transforming itself into a plebiscitary democracy. Here it does not much matter if the regime continues to use some of the language of constitutional government and appears to retain some constitutional arrangements. Substantively, the society is becoming wedded to the aims of its now preponderant character type and thus adopting new institutions.

Between the divergent larger purposes that acquire political form in a constitutional democracy and a plebiscitary democracy there is finally a radical dissonance. This does not mean that their mutually destructive ways cannot coexist for a time in particular societies. Indeed, constitutional democracy assumes the inevitable presence in society of political and other influences that are more or less destructive of its own higher purpose. A recognition of their inevitability is contained within its understanding of the higher end of politics and is reflected in the institutional means that it adopts to approximate the end. Yet, the institutions of constitutional democracy are endangered or destroyed in proportion as they are placed in the service of the plebiscitary personality.

Thinkers who are prone to distinguish between true ethical universality and the particularities of life tend to interpret theories of ethics and politics in the abstract, without sufficient attention to their concrete, experiential referents. At worst, a writer's use of particular terms is taken as evidence of his having predilections similar to those of thinkers who employ the same or similar terms. Jean-Jacques Rousseau's use of terms like "virtue," "justice," and "the common good" and his fondness for Greek examples might suggest an outlook similar to that of Plato or Aristotle. Or his stress on "pity" might be thought to indicate a moral outlook closely related to Christianity. As has been shown, the concrete substance of Rousseau's terms is sharply at odds with that of their apparent antecedents. His thought turns out to be in its main thrust a radical departure from the classical and Christian traditions.

Rousseau's thought illustrates well that concepts of ethical good reveal their real meaning only in the concrete patterns of action that they entail or imply. In Rousseau's political philosophy the common good is defined by the allegedly virtuous general will of the people. It should be carefully noted that its goodness is demonstrated by the fact that it abjures particular interests. For the citizens to become participants in the general will their social and political attachments must not be divided but belong entirely to the whole. In addressing public issues the citizens must not consider how possible legislative acts will affect particular groups in society towards which they might feel loyalty. On the contrary, group interests are by their very nature inimical to the general will. Genuine acts of popular sovereignty are unaffected by memberships. Rousseau takes great care in *The Social Contract* to purge society of influences that separate the citizen from the collective. He emphatically renounces sectional associations within the state. Virtuous popular decisions have as their sole source the undifferentiated mass of individuals. Rousseau is at the same time a radical individualist, one who wants to "liberate" the individual from particular associations, and a radical collectivist, one who makes the most comprehensive political whole into the only arena for virtuous human striving.[3]

It is essential to recognize that for Rousseau achieving the common good does not involve an accommodation of varying

---

3 See, in particular, Jean-Jacques Rousseau, *The Social Contract*, trans. Maurice Cranston (Harmondsworth: Penguin Books, 1968), Bk. II, Chap. III.

interests within society. The jockeying for influence by individuals and groups that characterizes all known politics is abhorrent to him and viewed as irrelevant to finding the right political course. Asserting the radical incompatibility of partisanship and the common good, he is in fact proclaiming the moral necessity of abolishing politics.

The substance of Rousseau's conception of the common good is thus disclosed in large part in his attack on particular interests and social loyalties. The significance of this analysis is perhaps more readily understood if Rousseau's preferences are contrasted with ones that are expressed by the American political tradition. In his report on the most striking characteristics of American society, Alexis de Tocqueville stressed the centrality of groups and associations. Americans exhibited a strong inclination to join together privately and locally to meet their own needs. Since American society was prone to place decisions in the hands of those most directly affected, it fostered highly decentralized social structures. The preference for leaving the initiative to the people immediately concerned kept political power under largely local control and the central government limited. Contrary to Rousseau's hatred of sectional associations and to his ideal of the undifferentiated mass as the agent for virtuous decisions, America has created an intricate and proliferating network of associations, interests and divided authority ranging from families, neighborhoods, churches and local communities to the Federal system and the constitutional structures of checks and balances.

Just as the concrete social and political aspirations of Rousseau manifest the substance of his ethical idealism, so do the traditional social and political structures of the United States give concrete form to a very different ethic. Whether by deliberate intent or spontaneous evolution, American tradition affirms that man develops his humanity through life in groups, through action that is intended primarily to affect circumstances within his own sphere of life. The presumption that people are mainly, if not exclusively, responsible for improving themselves and their own circumstances, for contributing through their own efforts to community among people with whom they come into personal contact, represents an old Western ethical tradition. That tradition is informed by the Christian admonition to "love neighbor." To shoulder responsibility for particular individuals at relatively close range who may be known to the person is very different from entertaining kindly feelings towards nobody in particular or towards people somewhere at a great distance. The latter involves striking a moral pose and requires little effort. The former demands specific and personally demanding actions, which is to say that it presupposes and fosters moral character of a certain kind.

The traditional Western ethic encourages social and political structures that enact or facilitate love of neighbor. Ethical universality is concretized in particulars of action and association that develop man's humanity. The ethical goal and the specific means, the form and the substance, are indistinguishable. The Rousseauistic ethic, in sharp contrast to the one exemplified by American tradition, does not seek embodiment in groups and corresponding concrete responsibilities. It reveals its essential nature by attacking them. The field of Rousseauistic virtue is a collective sphere emptied of the particular social obligations that require moral character in the traditional sense.

For laws to be in accordance with the general will, Rousseau explains, they must spring equally from all the citizens and apply equally to all of them. For this commonality of purpose to emerge society must rid itself of traditional inequalities and divisions. As long as citizens are shaped by groups and diverse conditions they will have diverse desires and be affected differently by legislative enactments, which will rob laws of their generality. While American traditional social and political structures assume the potential benefit to the common good of a great variety of interests and conditions, Rousseau views the common good as made possible by uniformity of purpose and condition. Man finds his moral identity in the all-encompassing, impersonal, undifferentiated collective—the general will.

Two notions of ethics and politics which employ partly similar terms thus reveal their sharply divergent meanings in the concrete social and political structures in which they are embodied. Constitutional and plebiscitary democracy are not two versions of essentially the same form of government but political manifestations of incompatible understandings of man's nature and purpose.

The Ethics of Freedom and Diversity

It might be objected that although Rousseau's notion of ethics in politics is questionable in its radical opposition to associations and social diversity, the proposed alternative ethic places undue stress on the possible legitimacy of particular interests. If some particular interests should be permitted, the extent to which they are legitimate could be determined only with reference to a standard that is independent of them. Unless ethical universality is above all partisanship and sets a clear standard in relation to which ethical progress can be assessed, society cannot be guided to the good of the whole. The view presented in this book seems to infect the common good with partisan bickering and leave it generally amorphous and directionless.

The habit of separating universality from historical particularity, though deeply rooted in Western thought, should be resisted, most generally because it perpetuates a tendency not to look for or seize the concrete moral opportunities of life. A fondness for an abstract model of perfection produces a certain disdain for the mundane actual conditions of life. This moral idealism predisposes the individual to a lack of resourcefulness in meeting moral challenges actually faced. The inclination to understand ethical good in abstract intellectual terms leads either to scornful withdrawal from imperfect politics or to efforts to force it into conformity with the moral ideal.

If it were true that there exists an ideal standard of the common good, a rational model of justice or a set of human rights, it would be consistent to discount or disregard the current particulars of human society. It would be the moral duty of persons knowledgeable about the ideal to imitate it, to decree its requirements and subject particular wills to virtuous direction. Human freedom and personal uniqueness would be irrelevant to the task of promoting the good society. What is needed is conformity to the standard. Indeed, from the point of view of an ahistorical notion of the common good, freedom, individuality and diversity appear as threats, for they introduce the complication of possible deviation from the ideal.

The present defense of particularity, including the interests of individuals and groups, does not undermine but affirms real ethical universality. It acknowledges an essential truth, that the transcendent value of ethical good has to be realized by particular human beings in the concrete circumstances of their lives. Not only do different generations and societies have different problems, but a myriad of diverse challenges have to be faced by individuals within the same generation or society. In order to respect the ethical imperative of his existence man does not have to flee from the changeability and particularity of history. On the contrary, he must pursue the value of ethical universality through them or miss it entirely. We are obligated to seize the moral opportunities of the here and now, to make the best of actual situations, however discouraging they may appear. As has been discussed earlier at length, human life is ultimately not ordered morally by precepts of reason that could be only tenuously related to specific circumstances. The ethical imperative is a special quality of will, a purposiveness within practical action that can inspire the ethical enhancement of an infinite number of different circumstances. The spirit of good has the power to affect all situations for the better, because it works not in the abstract, according to preconceived intellectual expectations, but upon the concrete and unique particulars of human choices. Although the ethical good is always the same in respect to the special quality of will that brings it into being, its concrete specifics are as changeable as the circumstances in which it must be effective.

The idea of universal norms discernible by human reason that are prior to and separate from all historical particularity assumes an ability to foresee the essentials of all circumstances. If the rational norms are really universal and always relevant, life must not contain any real surprises. Life must be to that extent static. Differently put, reason—at least the reason of the most enlightened—must be capable of virtual omniscience in the area of moral choice. Ethical rationalism typically acknowledges the existence of complex and unusual circumstances, but these are not thought to limit the capacity and reach of reason; particular cases can always be brought under the purview of universal principles through some form of casuistry. This intellectualistic view of ethical universality exaggerates our ability to capture in advance the specific moral requirements of all situations. More fundamentally, it fails to identify what is ultimately normative and neglects to take full account of the essential dynamism of human existence. The change and permanence of life are inextricably intertwined. To acquire a vital relation to actual moral choices ethical universality must be not applied to but synthesized with particularity. The universal must itself become concrete, the transcendent become immanent. The uniqueness that forms an integral part of all circumstances calls for creativity by those who have to act.

Innumerable choices need to be made throughout society, and the particular situations in which they take place all contain an ingredient of newness. Advancing the common good in politics requires among other things improvisation in the face of the wholly unexpected. The individuals ordinarily in the best position to decide are those most directly involved and most familiar with the circumstances at hand. Ethically responsible leaders at a distance from specific problems can aid by setting a special tone in society and by contributing such coordination and encouragement as is helpful, but sensitivity to the emerging ethical opportunities of particular situations can be induced only in small part by central political or intellectual authority. The needed moral acuity must be nurtured and practiced by individuals for themselves in the contexts of their own lives, even though their effort may be guided by authority and example.

Because the ethical good must be realized in concrete particulars by individuals who assert their will in circumstances best known to them, a variety of specific actions and objectives build up the purpose of ethical universality. The common good in politics is constituted by many interests, those particular interests that together advance the ethical life of society. Not even the most enlightened individuals could replace this historically evolving structure of human striving with their own intellectual direction. No one can survey, anticipate and comprehend the vast number of particular moral needs that have to be met by individual human beings throughout society.

Even if it were possible to purge politics of special interests, it would be highly undesirable. Among the special interests in society are more or less organized efforts that represent ethical will. What is ethically desirable is to structure society and government so that interests of a certain quality, those constitutive of moral community, are favored over others. The ethical purpose of constitutionalism is to encourage the proper self-restraint among competing individuals and groups and to make room for the proper discrimination between them by those who have power to encourage or discourage behavior. Constitutional arrangements are intended to restrain blatantly unethical partisanship and to make it easier for worthier aspirations to have an influence. What particular interests are ethically legitimate cannot be decided in the abstract and in advance, although naturally society must always have its more or less provisional preconceptions about what constitutes unseemly or wholly unacceptable partisanship.

The reason why a proliferation of interests and freedom of competition should be permitted and even fostered is that they are potentially of great benefit to the whole. New human aspirations should be allowed to present themselves in response to new circumstances and have a chance to convince of their benefit to an evolving common good. Partly because it cannot be predicted what concrete interests will promote the common good in particular historical circumstances, constitutional structures and corresponding social structures must not enforce overly rigid preconceptions. Without some considerable institutional flexibility and adaptability society will not accommodate the freshness and creativity of effort that is indispensable to the common good. New discoveries as to how life can best be lived are possible. Emerging opportunities may be seized in surprising ways by particular groups or individuals. Sometimes unexpected initiatives with the potential for greatly enriching and deepening the experience of civilization run afoul of convention and can be sustained only through individuals and groups with the courage and persistence to challenge established ways. The need for flexibility and tolerance is perhaps easiest to recognize in the artistic and intellectual realms, but it is no less important in the ethical life.

Most fundamentally, freedom and diversity are needed because universal values must be discovered anew by each generation and by each person. Universal values may be embodied in sound tradition, so that the citizens are guided towards realization of good by absorbing inherited ways. But this absorption, insofar as it is conducive to true universality, does not consist of an attempt simply to imitate or repeat the past. Universality must be incarnated in the circumstances of new generations and individuals. It must become a living, inspiring force in the present, which is to say that genuine universality is indistinguishable from human creativity. Sound traditions, whether in philosophy, the arts or ethics, are always threatened by conventional formalism, deadening routine, and entropy. It should also be underscored that not even the noblest and most vigorous conventions exhaust the ways in which universal values can be realized.

The Good as Historically Evolving

Universal values cannot be summed up in a particular code of conduct or model of perfection. In the end, they surpass all doctrinal articulations. The complexity and diversity of life defies intellectual efforts to prescribe the specifics of right conduct for all times and places. An inclination to identify the ethical good with "principles" and with diligent effort to implement them ignores the permanent need for creative adjustment to circumstance.

These remarks are not intended to disparage the role of reason in the ethical life, only to indicate that reason is not itself the ultimate, normative authority. As a moral being man finally defers to the authority of a higher will. Although not ethically normative, reason continuously seeks to *articulate* man's ethical experience. Philosophy gives conceptual, intellectual, definitional form to value realities already known in experience. Philosophy is in that sense historical. It studies the universal in the particular. The task of ethical philosophy is to take systematic account of the special purposiveness of man's higher will and of its relationship to other dimensions of human experience. Sound philosophy helps prepare the individual for moral action by theoretically articulating the meaning of action already performed. There is also another kind of reasoning, not primarily philosophical but pragmatic, that is integral and indispensable to the ethical life. This is the rationality that formulates principles and norms to guide conduct. This formulation involves simplification and reification of living moral reality, but it is a pragmatic necessity nevertheless. While the realization of ethical universality requires that particular principles be enunciated to help individuals keep or find their bearings, specific norms are transcended in the moment of choice by the ethical imperative itself. The unique situation calls for creative synthesis of the universal value and concrete particulars. The better a person's ethical philosophy and the more soundly inspired the principles at his disposal, the more favorable the circumstances for a moral resolution. But not even the very best "intellectual environment" ensures moral action. Always more or less tentative and provisional, principles of right conduct require continual interpretation and revision in the light of evolving moral experience.[4]

Universal value—be it moral, intellectual, or aesthetical—is revealed not in the abstract but in the continuing historical manifestations of the good, the true, and the beautiful. Sometimes these manifestations take society by surprise. New concrete acts of universality inspire men afresh or make them see life with new eyes. Universality is thus a historically evolving power disclosing its concrete nature in changing circumstances.

Ethical rationalism is not content with a notion of ethical universality that leaves the higher goal of society somehow open. It demands a specific, precise definition of the common good that real ethical universality does not offer. Ethical rationalism might say about a constitutional democracy that does not clearly declare its moral objectives that it is subject to the vagaries of historical chance and political opportunism. But, as should be clear, the refusal here to specify in formulas what constitutes the good society does not mean that the individual or society is left without definite moral guidance. All that it signifies is that what finally gives ethical structure to action takes a different form than codes of conduct (although codes can be helpful in advancing the ethical life).

A complaint that this understanding of ethical universality leaves the direction of morality vague is justified only insofar as the present argument denies that the specific substance of ethically desirable actions can be summed up in a statement of principles, rights, or the like. For reasons already given, such specifics cannot be decreed, except for pragmatic and

---

4 The relationship between reason and ethical will and the distinction between philosophical and pragmatic reason are treated at length in Ryn, *Will, Imagination and Reason*.

ceremonial purposes, without detriment to the ethical purpose of society. Also, this book puts more emphasis on the universal character of the ethical life than on its concrete particulars. A study that stressed the latter and marshaled a multitude of historical examples would obviously expand the sense of the concrete substance of morality. That it is possible to say a great deal about the concrete nature of society's higher end is evident already from the kind of philosophical reflection that is represented by this book. While ethical philosophy is ill served by codifying and schematic approaches that force the dynamics and complexities of the ethical life into neat formulae, a systematic account of the simultaneous tension and synthesis of universality and particularity describes a permanent structure of experience. This knowledge is also about the future in the sense that it refers to the human moral predicament at all times and in all places. From the point of view of desiring knowledge of the concrete direction of morality, the following is equally significant: Knowledge about the *form* of the ethical life in its different aspects is also knowledge about its concrete *substance,* the two being indistinguishable, although the future specifics of good action are unknown.

The fact that ethical universality must seek its aim in forever new concrete ways does not detract from the special purposive orientation that makes it distinctive or diminish its claim on our loyalty. On the contrary, it is precisely because the ethical good may become manifest in diverse concrete situations, including ones highly unfavorable to it, that its purpose can always be maintained. As a power seeking incarnation in the here and now, the real ethical imperative offers no excuse for shirking ethical responsibility. By comparison, an ethic of "principles," which typically finds that the present situation does not quite fit the most relevant regulative idea, creates a tendency not to act or to act with excessive rigidity.

In general, the abstract intellectual norm distracts the individual from the historical particulars and thus from the actual moral potentialities of the situation.

It is a serious flaw of ahistorical notions of ethical good that they do not recognize the potential moral purposiveness of practical action itself. The authority and direction of the ethical will emerge over time in the actions that it sanctions. To the extent that ethical universality becomes embodied in practice, it builds a historical record that shapes further action. A mighty structure of human striving, including political institutions, comes into being. The ethical will seeks to put all human activity, including philosophy, art, and economic production, in its service. The resulting structure as a whole reveals a lasting higher purpose. Ethical universality becomes known both by what it shuns and by what it sanctions. The awareness of ethical good that inheres in the experience of moral action is intrinsically authoritative. It is this quality of being that finally answers man's questions about what makes life worth living. The accumulating value of ethical action passes experiential judgment on action of a lower, morally detrimental kind and seeks to limit its sway. The fact that ethical universality becomes historically concrete in varying specifics does not mean that it is erratic or directionless. The opposite is the case. Its larger purpose is one and the same. But only through changing and diverse means can ethical universality maintain historical continuity through changing and diverse circumstances. It is the variability of moral effort that ensures the vitality of man's experience of the transcendent good.

Ethical universality is prior to all specific human actions in that it always wills that life should have a special quality. That quality has been described in this book in terms of community. Ethical conscience is a shared sense of higher purpose.

It sanctions certain incipient actions, censures others. It is possible to say in advance of particular choices that ethical conscience will censure whatever is destructive of the goal of moral community. To do so is its very nature. It is also possible to predict that the ethical imperative will inspire a search for actions that realize good in coming situations. What cannot be predicted are the specific approvals and disapprovals of ethical conscience.

In one sense, constitutional democracy as here understood does define the common good ahead of time. In its institutions and in the personality traits that it favors as necessary to sustain them over time it in effect proclaims a vision of what life ought to be. Although still needing the specificity of future actions, this vision is far from lacking in orientation. The kind of person who is required for the creation and continuation of constitutional democracy and who is most attuned to its ways of making decisions has such character traits as self-restraint, willingness to compromise, and tolerance of disagreement—dispositions that do not, however, extend to acceptance of the ignoble or exclude readiness to combat positive evil. Above all, the constitutional personality is sensitive to the needs of the common good and has the integrity and strength of will to press this higher purpose. As should be well understood by now, these qualities are not easily achieved and maintained on a large scale. Constitutional democracy is therefore easily lost. But where the constitutional personality, with all that it presupposes in regard to moral, intellectual and cultural preparation, is dominant, it exhibits preferences of a particular kind. These represent the direction of an entire civilization. The constitutional personality wants to enhance the strengths of that civilization and protect it against threats. While it is impossible to predict what specific choices will be made by such individuals in particular situations, their decisions will be inspired, insofar as they are true to their own higher self, by the ethical will. The choices to which it gives shape will reveal its enduring purpose in the given circumstances. The substance and direction of action are indistinguishable from its qualitative form. The historically emerging purposiveness of ethical universality is also revealed negatively by all of what it shuns. The specific content of its rejections cannot be predicted, but regardless of time and circumstances it will scorn the quality of action that is destructive of community—intolerance, lack of self-restraint, unwillingness to compromise, but also any inclination not to do what is necessary to constrain or defeat evil. Most generally, the ethical imperative is known as shunning a lack of ethical sensitivity. Such a statement of ethical universality is in a sense tautological, and must be. It elaborates what is already contained within the term "ethical." But this tautology can be fully recognized as such only if the concrete experiential reality of moral negativity with a positive purpose is recognized.

The fact that the common good is changing and evolving thus does not detract from its purposive nature. The "vagueness" regarding the specifics of the common good, while it may bother proponents of a rationalistic ethic of principles, is due to the variability and unpredictability of life itself.

Ethical Realism

The explanation of the purposiveness of ethical universality has perhaps seemed at times to assume that the actions of some individuals or groups embody an ethical purpose and nothing else and that the actions of some others are inspired by selfishness and nothing else. To avoid any misunderstanding it should perhaps be stated explicitly that such an impression is not intended. Though people vary greatly in character and some achieve ethical nobility while others sink to the level of the diabolical, the duality of higher and lower potentialities marks all of human nature. This view of man's predicament is essential to the understanding of how ethical universality becomes embodied in historical action. It has particular significance for the theory of constitutionalism.

Man's ethical responsibility belongs to the world of human imperfections and perversities, not to an abstract ideal sphere. The individual must try to make the best of actual situations, even those that seem not at all conducive to good. Truly ethical action does not proceed as if foul motives and behavior did not exist. It takes their chronic presence in society into account in selecting its means. It even tries as far as possible to make use of human immorality and other weaknesses for its own purpose. Disregarding or minimizing obstacles in the setting of goals is contrary to ethical responsibility, for it threatens the limited moral progress that is possible. To approach politics in disregard of the ignoble or in anticipation of its eventual disappearance from the world is not only utopian but immoral.

Deriving methods and goals from a purely abstract ideal of perfection is destructive of the ethical life. Thinkers or statesmen who are disinclined to take the world as it is and to look for the moral opportunities it actually offers may view constitutionalism as compromising the highest moral standards. But high-sounding principles that bear no direct relationship to concrete historical realities and potentialities mask avoidance of the task at hand. It may be retorted that modesty of aim is no virtue. If by modesty is meant a relaxation of ethical effort, the comment is valid. But constitutionalism as here understood does not represent a dilution or lowering of the moral objective. The opposite is the case. Constitutional democracy represents an effort to achieve as much good as is possible within particular political circumstances. Building constitutional restraints and purposive structures into popular government is to heed both higher and lower human potentialities. Without fully considering human limitations and letting them affect the understanding of what lies within the realm of the possible, there can be no realistic pursuit of the common good. Constitutionalism can be said to accommodate man's weaknesses, but that accommodation does not constitute a relaxation of moral responsibility. Modesty of aim in the sense of adjusting ends and means to actual possibilities is of the essence of genuine ethical action. The moral credentials of moral idealism, by comparison, are highly questionable. Its disembodied standards do not well prepare man for actually advancing the common good.

Constitutional democracy exemplifies the way in which ethical realism seeks to shape particular political and historical conditions to its own end. Without the kind of constitutional arrangements and corresponding personality traits that have been described, popular government will undermine the ethical purpose of society.

The State of Democracy XIV

To write of the ethical potentialities of Western democracy in the closing years of the twentieth century may be to write about missed opportunities. It is an open question today whether constitutional democracy will be able to maintain itself into the next century. There are many signs that its ethical, intellectual and cultural foundations are eroding. One of the effects of a historical understanding of ethics and politics is to sharpen the awareness of the origins and preconditions of particular social and political arrangements. Forms of government are only partially the result of intellectual design. Even when extensive deliberation goes into the shaping of a political regime the larger currents of history have a powerful influence that is not even fully discernible by those who live at the time. To some extent, the flow of history gives to formulated plans a different meaning in practice than could be anticipated. While the stability of a successful form of government may be due in considerable part to the wisdom of the intellectual effort behind it, much besides the articulated principles of the regime account for its actual historical existence. The wisdom of the plans is itself historically derived in large measure. Only intellectual superficiality would attribute great insight to an abstract, self-generating and autonomous reason possessed by individuals in isolation.

Taking the U.S. Constitution as an example, the written document was but one element in a large, complex, and still emerging historical whole, part of which was not known or was known only intuitively by the authors. There is a sense in which an unwritten constitution sustains or overwhelms any written document. Historically evolved conditions and predilections covering a wide range of human concerns provided the hospitable soil for the constitutional arrangements proposed in 1787.[1] A particular civilized heritage made possible the eventual emergence of constitutional democracy. It is not clear that at the opening of the twenty-first century the ethical and cultural prerequisites for constitutional democracy will be present. A telling sign that democracy is in danger, and is threatened by self-destruction, is the frantic and uncritical manner in which democracy is proclaimed and extolled.

Constitutional democracy may be the most demanding form of government imaginable. It can function over time only if most of the citizens, and not just political leaders, have a high degree of moral character and circumspection. The ethical, cultural and intellectual prerequisites of constitutional democracy make it difficult to achieve and maintain. Today, it is increasingly evident that American constitutionalism is being transformed into something far removed from the hopes and expectations of the framers of the Constitution. The current practices of American democracy illustrate how the concrete substance of political action says more about the nature of institutions than official governing documents or other language describing the government. More and more, American

---

1 The origins of the American constitutional order in Hebrew, Greek, Roman, Christian and early modern civilization are summarized in Russell Kirk, *The Roots of American Order* (La Salle, Ill.: Open Court, 1974). See also Forrest McDonald, *Novus Ordo Seclorum. The Intellectual Origins of the Constitution* (Lawrence, Kansas: University Press of Kansas, 1985).

politics exhibits the patterns and preferences of plebiscitary democracy. Majoritarian and quantitative considerations are prominent both in the theory and practice of politics. It is widely assumed that the task of government is to implement the wishes of the current numerical majority. Much of the effort of elected officials and aspiring politicians is devoted to securing a majority or plurality in the next election. A vast expansion and centralization of government has come about in the name of serving the people. A huge and burgeoning government bureaucracy is intricately intertwined with expanding bureaucracies in business, education, and other fields.

Seeing American constitutionalism in jeopardy, people with an ahistorical understanding of politics may argue for a return to "the principles" of the Constitution. But not even the most persuasive reasoning about their strengths could, by itself, restore the ethical spirit of constitutionalism. It is poorly understood that traditional American constitutional structures contained and presupposed far more than is expressed in any text. They were specific manifestations of larger ethical and cultural preferences, and these are now gradually disappearing. In the absence of strong and sustained efforts to reconstruct or reconstitute the civilized setting of constitutional arrangements, no amount of fervent abstract defense of principle can revivify constitutional democracy.

Many developments in modern American society, with counterparts in other Western democracies, indicate the evanescence of the civilization of which the constitutional personality is a part. A wide range of social and political problems are symptomatic of a fading of character traits and other proclivities which made constitutional democracy possible. Celebrations of economic, technical, medical and other advances cannot conceal the scope and depth of democracy's deterioration. The following litany of problems could easily be extended.

In the world's leading democracy the rule of law and order has become so uncertain and fragile that a sense of insecurity among the citizens is taken for granted. Criminality is epidemic and often characterized by extraordinary callousness. In many places criminals compete successfully with government for control. Most crimes go unpunished. The failure of government to deal effectively with threats to the life and limb of the citizens exemplifies a general permissiveness and lack of conviction about the stated purposes of society. This failure is also symptomatic of a larger transformation of the role and meaning of law. The special dignity that once attached to the law as an impartial norm serving the common good is being lost. The law is perceived more and more as an instrument used by economic, ethnic or ideological pressure groups to advance flagrantly self-serving objectives. At the same time that courts and lawyers are inserting themselves into ever new fields of social life, the legal system is marked by growing unpredictability and arbitrariness, many examples of which have been provided by Supreme Court decisions that blatantly violate the spirit of the Constitution. The decline of the law is a significant cause of a more or less articulate feeling among the citizens that they are subject to capricious manipulation.

Traditional social norms and mores are eroding. The family is losing its cohesion and its centrality as a source of personal growth and a transmitter of values. Standards of personal behavior and deportment are low and declining. The disappearance of an older sexual morality produces rank promiscuity and epidemics of AIDS and venereal disease. Abortions are performed routinely and in staggering numbers. Drug abuse is rampant. Honesty and integrity lose ground to shadiness and opportunism. Workmanship is poor. The capacity for self-discipline and sustained effort is withering away. The cultural prominence of entertainment and diversions expresses and encourages a flight from real obligations and problems. In academia and education generally the humane center of learning is virtually lost. In its stead, ideological postures and fads set the intellectual and moral tone. Low academic standards are advocated by many educators themselves. Celebrity status, "visibility," and journalistic skill confer authority. An obsession with news replaces a concern for lasting truth and wisdom. The rights and freedoms of the press are given cultic proportions. In the arts, a collapse of aesthetical judgment has led to acceptance and high praise for the trivial, the weird, the silly, the vulgar, and the morbid. Representatives of organized religion place little or no emphasis on sin or the need for repentance but turn religion and ethics into a sentimental ritual of "compassion." The breakdown of an older sense of proportion, self-restraint and order of priorities is reflected in obtrusive commercialism and consumerism. Some of what is tolerated in the marketplace and in commercially thriving popular culture would have horrified earlier generations. In sports, even tennis has been invaded by bad-mannered misfits who, only decades ago, would have been barred instantly from competition. Throughout society, a seemingly boundless tolerance of whatever denigrates traditional civilization chips away at lingering norms. Democracy seems headed for the triumph of the lowest common denominator.

In politics, the quality of leadership is declining. Persons of high character, genuine insight and capacity for directing others are exceedingly rare and have great difficulty advancing to positions of influence in a political and journalistic climate increasingly marked by superficiality and short-sightedness. Political responsibility and enlightened discourse are crowded

out by opportunism and sloganeering. The intensifying plebiscitary pressures, which are aggravated by media attention,
make politicians increasingly blatant in their pandering to the
voters and to those in journalism who present them to their
constituencies and can shape their reputations. Successful
politicians tend to be browbeaten and insecure individuals
lacking in deeper convictions. Violating the opinions favored
by the electronic and print media is potentially devastating to
their careers. Various real and serious problems are either ta-
boo or mentionable only in oblique and roundabout ways. Inherited representative institutions have been so transformed
by plebiscitary practices that they provide little protection for
leaders of integrity and courage who would run the risk of
deviating from currently dominant opinion in order to serve
the higher good of the people. Hypocrisy abounds. While democracy and the wisdom of the people are lauded, candidates
for office show in their election campaigns that they actually
assume the electorate to be both foolish and ignorant.

Is further evidence needed to show that the constitutional
personality and the civilization from which it is indistinguishable are retreating? A listing of more encouraging signs and
developments would add some nuance and balance to this di-
agnosis of the state of democracy, but it would not dispel the
impression of pervasive decline. That constitutional democracy is deteriorating at its ethical core can be seen from the
fact that those who still speak the language of moral obligation
and the common good are usually espousing beliefs far removed from the traditional emphasis on character and self-
restraint. They also tend to identify morality with laws,
rights, or rules, giving morality legalistic connotations. Mor-
alists of this orientation judge the morality of behavior according to its adherence to or deviation from formal principle. Up-
holding morality falls increasingly to legislators, courts,

lawyers, and academic casuists, and to administrative bodies
that intrude further and further into the lives of the citizens.
The general direction of decrees is set by ideological fashion.
Private and public action is subject to inquisitorial scrutiny,
and a steady stream of new rules and guidelines are proposed
to deal with alleged injustice or wrongdoing. Thus is the disappearance of the substance of moral character made evident
in an epidemic of moralistic legalism.

Many people, perhaps especially in the United States, assume Western democracy to be in good health and to represent the wave of the future for the rest of the world. Sentiments of that type are usually so lacking in realism and
intellectual stringency as to be themselves compelling evidence of the precarious state of Western democracy. They signify a more or less conscious flight from serious problems that
are undermining not only constitutional popular government
but civilized life itself.

It has been argued here that ethical universality must seek
its course in given historical circumstances. What lies within
the realm of the possible for Western democracy today is a
matter of more or less well-informed conjecture. Although
the present difficulties of democracy are severe and seemingly
life-threatening, it is conceivable that constitutional democracy could be reinvigorated through extraordinary ethical, intellectual, cultural and political effort. Besides other changes,
substantial modifications of existing political practices are
necessary to save the constitutional order. Rousing the Western world from its complacency and reversing present trends
would require strong, imaginative, and courageous leadership. The spirit of the age will strike ruthlessly against any
real challenges to its authority.

But it would be a sign of moral and intellectual escapism
not also to contemplate the prospect of a continued decline of

Western civilization, and the possibility of great calamities to come. Perhaps a recovery of realism will have to await some fearsome world events or stark domestic consequences of irresponsibility. Present plebiscitary trends and related developments are destroying democracy from within. A bureaucratic "soft" despotism, observing various democratic formalities and justifying its centralizing and expansive projects as doing the work of the people, may be able for some time to maintain a selective, externally imposed order at the same time that the traditional social fabric disintegrates. Perhaps domestic instability or threatening international events will, in the end, generate dictatorial rule in some Western countries. In the United States, acute dangers or fears may give rise to a great surge of extra-constitutional presidential power. Whatever the most likely outcome, moral, intellectual, and cultural conditions in the Western world today force serious thinkers to reckon with the sad possibility of constitutional democracy's final demise. It is necessary to consider by what realistic means the ethical life can be protected and sustained in historical circumstances that conspire against it.

Index

Anarchy: Rousseau's longing for, 102; in Rousseau's state of nature, 105; effect in practice of Rousseau's teaching, 150

Animal symbolicum, defined, 36–42

Arbitrariness: restrained by law, 15, 166–67, 171, 174, 179; unleashed by utopianism, 149; negated by spirit of constitutionalism, 172, 179

Aristotle: on prudence and morality, 72; on happiness, 76–80, 82n; on true friendship, 84; on habit and virtue, 87, 96, 126; contrasted with Rousseau, 137, 163; mentioned, 8, 9, 30, 38n

Aron, Raymond, 194n

Autonomous groups: prohibited by Rousseau, 128, 138–39, 215–218; defined by Nisbet, rejected by Rousseau, endorsed by Burke, 139; supported by U.S. Constitution, 190, 216–18; threatened by majoritarianism, 191; need for in democracy, 195–96, 215–23

Babbitt, Irving: on dualism, 58–59; on inner check, 70, 82n, 85n; on Rousseau, 95, 147n, 197, 198; on humility and leadership, 202

Bachrach, Peter, 196–97

Behavioralism, 28

Bentley, Arthur, 29

Brecht, Arnold, 4

Buchanan, James, 24n

Burke, Edmund: on need for change, 88; compared to Rousseau, 139; on need for restraint, 150, 172–73, 181n; on representation, 184; on social affections, 196

Burnham, James, 190

Burns, James MacGregor: critical of U.S. Constitution, 186–87; on Jeffersonian model, 187–88; related to Rousseau, 190–93

Buytendijk, F. J. J., 37n

Calhoun, John C.: on constitutionalism, 168–70; constitutional theory of related to moral life, 176–77

Cassirer, Ernst: on animal symbolicum, 36–37, 39, 58n, 99n, 103n; on problem of community in Rousseau, 106; on ethical conscience in Rousseau, 133

Charvet, John, 133, 114

Checks and balances: and Madisonian tradition, 21; as restraint on majority, 155–60; related to Calhoun, 169; Burns's impatience with, 188

Civilization: as ultimate goal, 5; defined, 82; intrinsic value of, 85; need of change, 88; as seen by Rousseau, 102, 150; embodied in history, 227; as related to constitutional personality, 228–29; as setting for constitutional democracy, 234

Community: as seen by Dewey, 17; by Nisbet, 19; based on ethical con-

Community (*continued*)
science, 76, 83; as goal of social life,
83; definition of, 83–85; as end of
politics, 162; and popular sovereignty, 164; and freedom, 164–65,
218–23; and spirit of constitutionalism, 194; and autonomous groups,
195–96, 219–23; and revitalization
of democratic theory, 198; promoted
by representation, 199–200; embodied in the particular, 221–23
Concurrent majority, 170
Conscience. *See* Ethical conscience
Consensus: as prerequisite of government action, 160; promoted by U.S.
Constitution, 182; criticized by
Burns, 187
Constitutional democracy: defined, 13–
16, 93, 154, 193–94, 212; deficient
theories of, 11; contrasted with plebiscitary democracy, 15, 93, 193,
212–14; most demanding form of
government, 233; in jeopardy in
U.S., 233–39; as ethical realism,
166–72, 230–31
Constitutional personality: defined,
193, 228–29; basis of constitutional
democracy, 214; fading in U.S., 234–
38
Conway, Margaret, 31*n*
Croce, Benedetto, 23–24, 61*n*, 82*n*
Crocker, Lester, 140–41

Dahl, Robert: on decentralization, 195;
favoring "democratization," 196–97;
mentioned, 3*n*, 11
Deliberation: moral dimension of, 15;
moral need for, 71, 181; type desired
by Rousseau, 133; and morality, 177;
premium on in U.S. Constitution,
182
Dewey, John: on ends and means, 5–6,
12; on democracy as way of life, 17–
19, 42
Downs, Anthony: 3*n*, 11, 42*n*
Durbin, E. F. M., 3*n*
Durkheim, Emile, 105
Duverger, Maurice, 41–42

Easton, David: on goal of political science, 29–30; mentioned, 3*n*
Eliot, T. S., 57*n*
Ends and means: as seen by Mayo, 5;
by Dewey, 5–6; related to democracy,
5–8; as seen by Thorson, 12; by
Croce, 23–24
Equality: as basis of morality in Rousseau, 109–11, 114; abstract nature of
in Rousseau, 124; political goal for
Dahl and Bachrach, 197
Ethical conscience: defined, 8–9, 14,
20, 21, 23, 25, 49, 52, 54–56, 62–89
passim, 149–50, 176–78, 227–28; as
principle of community, 85; as seen
by Rousseau, 133, 136–37; as potential threat to the state, 140–41; as
dimension of constitutionalism, 172–
74. *See* Ethical universality
Ethical rationalism: exemplified, 209,
209*n*; weakness of, 211, 219, 227; its
neglect of creativity, 220–21, 223–
24; its demand for definition of good,
225
Ethical realism: need for, 20–26; lack
of in Rousseau, 108–111, 148–51;
and constitutionalism, 166–72; as integral to ethical responsibility, 208–
9, 229–31
Ethical universality: and "principles,"
206–7; and particular interests, 207;
embodied in the concrete, 211–12,
218–20; and creativity, 220–23; as
historical, 223–29; as negative and
positive, 69–73, 176–81, 225–229.
See Ethical conscience
Executive: function of in *Social Contract*, 120–22; role of as seen by
Burns, 188–91

Fact-value distinction: 1–50 *passim*,
46–48
Feigert, Frank, 31*n*
Foerster, Norman, 57*n*
Freedom: known in experience, 34;
moral paradox of, 73–75; Rousseau's
obsession with, 99, 144–45; of Rous-

seau's general will, 112; defined 164–65; ethics of, 218–223

Freud, Sigmund, 64n

Gehlen, Arnold, 37n, 40

General will: defined, 13–14, 92–151; as political, 95; as freedom, 111–12; based on equality, 113–14; defining morality, 117; distinguished from will of all, 118; incompatible with representation, 121; incompatible with constitutional restraints, 127–28, 134, 140; spontaneity of, 131–33; as totalitarian, 138; Spartan dimension of, 142–43; utopian nature of, 149; in practice, 150–51; threatened by life in groups, 214–18

Hallowell, John: on moral restraint in politics, 171, 175; on democracy and authority, 201; mentioned, 12

Happiness: defined by Aristotle, 77–80; by Plato, 78; communal value of, 80

Hegel, G. F., 59

Hendel, Charles W., 98n

Higher law: constitution as approximation of, 171; constitution as manifestation of, 175; constitutions subject to, 175; obedience to, 199–200; deficiency of legalistic conception of, 224–26, 237–38

Higher self: defined by Babbitt and More, 62–63; of a people, 163

Hobbes, Thomas: on morality and power, 20; criticized by Rousseau, 104; compared to Rousseau, 142

Impulse: defined, 65; in Rousseau, 132. See Spontaneity

Inner check, 63, 70, 57n

James, William, 29

Jefferson, Thomas: as plebiscitarian, 183–87; view of human nature, 186

Jeffersonian model, 187

Kant, Immanual, 124

Kelson, Hans, 3–4

Kendall, Willmoore: on U.S. Constitution and majoritarianism, 159–60; critical of Burns, 189

Kirk, Russell, 88, 233n

Kriszat, G., 37n

Langer, Susanne, 36–39

Leander, Folke, 57n, 61n

Lincoln, Abraham, 155

Lippmann, Walter: on constitutional restraints on arbitrariness, 171; and search for higher law, 175; mentioned, 12, 57n, 210n

Locke, John, 186n

Love of neighbor: moral significance of, 217

Lower self: defined by Babbitt and More, 62–63; of a people, 163

Machiavelli, Nicolo: on politics as power, 20; deficiency of, 22–23

MacIntyre, Alasdair, 210n

Madison, James, 21

Madisonian model: modifying conflict, 21; criticized by Burns, 187

Majoritarianism: moral deficiency of, 10, 181; of Rousseau, 128; thwarted by U.S. Constitution, 155–58; contrasted with Calhoun's concurrent majority, 170; of Jefferson, 183–86; of Burns, 186–93

Masson, P. M., 147n

Masters, Roger, 96n

Mayo, Henry B., 5–13 passim

McDonald, Forrest, 233n

McIlwain, Charles, 181n

Meyerhoff, Hans, 37n

Militarism: Rousseau's liking for, 100; of general will, 141–45

Mill, John Stuart, 16

Monism: of Hegel, 59; of Rousseau's view of human nature, 136–38

Moral freedom, 73–75, 164–65

More, Paul Elmer: on higher and lower self, 62–64; on flux and inner check, 68–69, 70, 110n; mentioned, 57

Morgenthau, Hans, 194n

Murray, John Courtney, 12
Murry, John M., 199–200

Nationalism: favored by Rousseau, 100; of general will, 141–45
Neibuhr, Reinhold: on self-transcendence, 39, 194*n*; on moral checks and democratic government, 201; mentioned, 12
Nihilism: in democratic theory, 8; dogmatism of, 48–49, 55, 68; obstacle of intellectual renewal, 198. *See* Relativism
Nisbet, Robert: on Rousseau, 95; compared to Rousseau, 139; on autonomous groups, 195–96; mentioned, 19

Paine, Thomas, 181
Particularity: as embodiment of the ethical, 210–18
Plato: on dualism, 57; and body-soul distinction, 60, 78, 79, 96, 127, 171; mentioned, 8, 9, 24
Plebiscitary democracy: of Rousseau, 13; defined, 93, 193, 212–13; utopian basis of in Rousseauism, 151, 154, 180, 192–93; roots of in Jefferson, 183–86; favored by Burns, 186–93; by Dahl and Bachrach, 196–97; contrasted with constitutional democracy, 212–214; gaining ground in U.S., 233–39. *See* Majoritarianism and Checks and balances
Popular sovereignty: in Rousseau, 112, 126, 127, 138; analyzed, 160–61; deficiency of Rousseau's concept of, 161
Portmann, Adolf, 37*n*
Procedural democracy, 3–7, 10–12
Publius, 158

Relativism: as basis of democracy, 3–4; as scientific, 4–5; criticized, 5–7, 48–49, 55, 68; fear of, 209. *See* Nihilism
Representation: rejected by Rousseau, 121–27; endorsed by Publius, 158; as viewed by Burke, 184; mistrusted by

Jefferson, 184–85; Dahl's ambiguous view of, 197; moral prerequisite of, 200; moral necessity of, 200–201; related to spirit of constitutionalism, 202–203
Riker, William, 42*n*
Ross, Alf, 11
Rommen, Heinrich, 210*n*
Rousseau, Jean-Jacques: father of democratic theory, 13–15, 49; romanticism of, 14, 90–100; political philosophy of, 92–151; on civil society, 102–103, 112–13; and unity of the people, 161, 164, 180, 183; compared to Jefferson, 186; compared to Burns, 190–93; his hostility to groups, 138–39, 214–18
Ryn, Claes, 210*n*, 225*n*

Sartori, Giovanni, 11
Scheler, Max, 37*n*, 40
Schumpeter, Joseph, 3
Self-interest: as preponderant force in politics, 20–22, 109, 168, 179, 181, 230; turned into service of common good, 22, 24, 86, 109–11, 170, 230–31; enlightened, 24–25, 42, 65, 169, 172, 207–208
Self-love: in Rousseau's state of nature, 104; basis of Rousseau's morality, 114–15, 135–36
Shklar, Judith, 97
Social contract: remedy for existing ills, 107; basis for social freedom and morality, 111–13
Sorauf, Frank, 44
Spirit of constitutionalism: defined, 172–75, 179–80, 194, 196; related to leadership, 202–203; and inevitability of selfishness, 208
Spontaneity: as source of morality in Rousseau, 13, 94, 132–34, 136; as potentially arbitrary, 15, 64, 149; man's detachment from, 39–41; ordered by moral will, 63; participating in moral purpose, 72; compatible with social discipline in Rousseau, 132; ambiguous term, analyzed, 177–

79; of moral sense in Jefferson, 186;
Burns's implied belief in, 190–91; in
plebiscitary democracy, 193. *See* Impulse
Stanlis, Peter, 210*n*
State of nature: described, 102–106;
ambiguity of, 103–104; of public person, 112; similar to Hobbes's concept, 142
Strauss, Leo, 47*n*, 107, 210*n*
Subjectivism: and the need to transcend, 8, 43–46, 48; alleged basis of
conscience, 54, 68; of Rousseau's
philosophy, 146–47

Taylor, Charles, 47*n*
Taylor, John, 184, 185*n*
Thomists, 209*n*
Thorson, Thomas L., 11, 12
Tillich, Paul, 40, 53*n*
Tingsten, Herbert, 11
Tocqueville, Alexis de, 155, 216
Tradition: and support of ethical life,
87–89, 138; denounced by Rousseau,
150; political order resting on, 201–202
Transcendence: ignored in democratic
theory, 3–8; of self, 39; of ethical

conscience, 9, 12, 46, 52, 55–56,
68, 173, 178; as dimension of existence, 57; seen as threat by Rousseau, 127, 140; of ethical will in relation to constitutions, 174; of
community, 198; of statesman's
cause, 202
Truman, David, 3*n*
Tullock, Gordon, 24*n*

Uexküll, J. v., 37*n*
Undifferentiated mass: favored by
Rousseau, 138–39, 190, 213, 215–18; negated by traditional Western
ethic, 216–17
Utopianism: of Rousseau, 99–101,
110–11, 131, 146, 148–51, 192–93;
of discounting leadership, 200

Value-centered historicism, 210–11
Viereck, Peter, 190*n*
Voegelin, Eric, 47*n*

Warnock, Mary, 73*n*
Warren, Austin, 57*n*
Williamson, René de Visme, 3*n*, 199–200

DATE DUE

~~JY 31 '81~~			
MR 2 92			
MY 4 '92			
~~MAR 16 200~~			
~~OCT 18 2001~~			

DEMCO 38-297